215-307-3918

MODERN WORLD NATIONS

Nigeria

Douglas A. Phillips

Series Consulting Editor
Charles F. Gritzner
South Dakota State University

CHELSEA HOUSE
PUBLISHERS
A Haights Cross Communications Company

Philadelphia

Frontispiece: Flag of Nigeria

Cover: Roofs in central Ibidan, Nigeria.

CHELSEA HOUSE PUBLISHERS

VP, NEW PRODUCT DEVELOPMENT Sally Cheney
DIRECTOR OF PRODUCTION Kim Shinners
CREATIVE MANAGER Takeshi Takahashi
MANUFACTURING MANAGER Diann Grasse

Staff for NIGERIA

EXECUTIVE EDITOR Lee Marcott
PRODUCTION EDITOR Megan Emery
PICTURE RESEARCHER 21st Century Publishing and Communications, Inc.
COVER DESIGNER Keith Trego
SERIES DESIGNER Takeshi Takahashi
LAYOUT 21st Century Publishing and Communications, Inc.

A Haights Cross Communications ◀━ Company

http://www.chelseahouse.com

First Printing

1 3 5 7 9 8 6 4 2

Library of Congress Cataloging-in-Publication Data

Phillips, Douglas A.
  Nigeria / by Douglas A. Phillips.
    p. cm. — (Modern world nations)
Includes index.
Summary: Describes the history, geography, government, economy, people, and culture of
Nigeria.
  ISBN 0-7910-7475-7
  1. Nigeria—Juvenile literature. [1. Nigeria.] I. Title. II. Series.
  DT515.22.P48 2003
  966.9—dc22

                                                                2003014158

Table of Contents

Nigeria

The Niger River runs through the heart of this country of 130 million people, and provides vital hydroelectric power, industrial transportation, drinking water, and irrigation for crops.

1

Introducing Nigeria

Incongruous. Some things in Nigeria just don't seem to make sense to the casual outside observer. For example, why does a leading oil-producing country have gas shortages and long lines at gas stations that may or may not have gas? Why did Nigeria have hundreds of deaths, second only to the United States, after the September 11, 2001, Al Qaida attacks on the Pentagon and World Trade Centers? Why is Osama bin Laden portrayed as a hero with his picture on cars in northern Nigeria? Incongruous, but that is Nigeria!

Nigeria is a tropical land located in West Africa. It extends from about 4° to 14° north latitude, with a north–south span of about 700 miles (1,125 kilometers). In an east–west direction, the country extends from roughly 3° to 13° east longitude, also a distance of about 700 miles. The country's total area of some 357,000 square miles (925,000 square kilometers)—slightly larger than Texas and Oklahoma combined—is, therefore, quite compact in shape.

The country's hot and soggy southern border faces upon the equatorial Gulf of Guinea (on the Atlantic Ocean). In the north, Nigeria extends into the Sahel region, nearly reaching the parched Sahara Desert. The country is surrounded on three sides by former French colonies. It sits alone, like an island, in this region as the sole former British possession. To the west is the country of Benin and to the north and northwest is Niger. Nigeria also shares a short border with Chad in the northeast and a much longer boundary with Cameroon to the east. The country's name comes from the Niger River, the country's major inland water feature. This river runs through the heart of Nigeria as it flows into the Gulf of Guinea. The Niger provides much of the country's hydroelectric power and also provides water for domestic use, industry, and irrigation.

Nigeria's history is filled with twists and turns that have taken it from tribal kingdoms to a British colony, from a colony to a military dictatorship, and from a dictatorship to a developing democracy visited and praised by then-U.S. President Bill Clinton. Nigeria's candle of democracy, however, is very fragile. The flame can easily be extinguished by ominous threats such as corruption, violence, and ethnic divisions, as was once again illustrated during elections held in the spring of 2003. According to the 1997 survey by Transparency International, a Berlin-based organization, Nigeria is the most corrupt of the world's 52 most-populated countries. A visitor may even encounter the problem of corruption upon arriving at the Lagos airport when an official asks for a gift.

Violence is no stranger to Nigeria. A recent news headline in one of the world's largest cities, Lagos, Nigeria, announced that police in the city had killed over 780 robbers during a 10-month period. Many were executed by firing squads. During the same span of time, 82 police officers were killed in the line of duty in Lagos. In late 2001, ethnic violence between

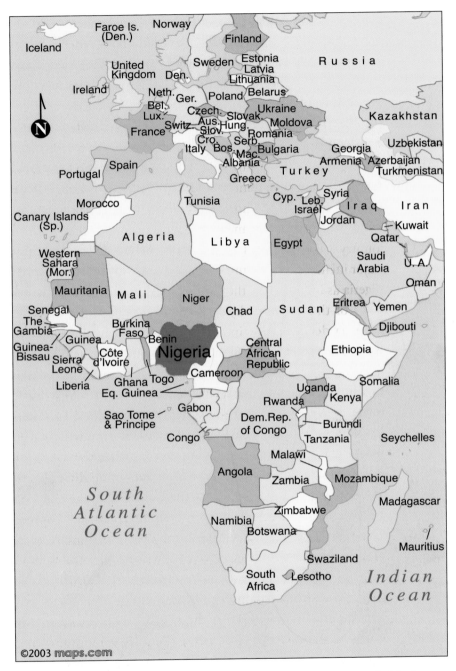

Located in Western Africa, Nigeria is a former British colony surrounded by former French colonies. Its location on the Atlantic Ocean has provided benefits for its modern economy.

Muslims and Christians in northern Nigeria was responsible for the deaths of hundreds of people and a similar event happened during 2002. Such ethnic violence has been a sad part of Nigeria's heritage. The candle of democracy is therefore very fragile in Nigeria—but it is still lit.

Nigeria was a British colony before gaining its independence on October 1, 1960. British influence is still evident in many ways, English is the national language and the educational system continues to be based on many British practices. Nigeria is a member of the Commonwealth of Nations composed of many former British colonies.

Nigeria is also the most populated nation in Africa with an estimated 130 million people. It is the world's ninth most populated country, ranking ahead of Mexico. This population translates into an average of over 350 people per square mile (217 per square kilometer). This density is four times greater than that of the United States. The population is also very diverse, with nearly 250 different languages being spoken. English serves as the national language, and perhaps more importantly, it serves to unite the country with a common language to allow for dialog between diverse populations. The most significant ethnic groups are the Hausa and Fulani in the north, and the Yoruba, Ibo, and Edo in the south. These groups will be explored in greater depth in Chapter 6.

Religion plays a huge role in the incongruence of Nigeria. The two main religions, Islam and Christianity, are each practiced by close to half of the country's people. This split in religious beliefs and practices has sometimes led to horrible religious clashes. Islam is predominant in the north and Christianity is prevalent in the south. Recently, 12 of the northern states where Islam is prevalent have adopted Sharia law. Sharia is a very strict form of Islamic law that, for example, has condemned women to death in Nigeria for adultery.

The variety of Christian faiths is great. Denominations range from the Anglican Church left by the British to the

Multiple wives and large families can mean many mouths to feed. Children sometimes work all day to help support the family and cannot go to school.

Catholic Church. There also are hundreds of new churches with names like Deeper Life Bible Church, Voice of Rapture Mission, Victorious Life Church, and the Heroes of Faith Ministries. These faiths combine Christianity with the cultures of Nigeria and often include enthusiastic singing, praying, and dancing in their religious services. Other indigenous religions, various animist faiths, make up the other 10 percent of the population of Nigeria.

Poverty is also an important problem facing Nigerians. In the 1970s, Nigeria had the thirty-third highest per person income in the world. Today the country is one of the world's poorest. The United Nations Human Development Index ranks Nigeria the twenty-ninth least livable country in the world. Life is very difficult here and most Nigerians struggle to make ends meet. Many families have their children selling things on the street or working in other ways to help the family survive. This means that youngsters are often not in school, a situation that creates other problems. The nation's literacy rate, for example, is only a dismal 57 percent.

The poverty creates other tragic stories that emerge in newspapers about desperate Nigerians breaking into oil pipelines to get fuel for cooking with horrible results of explosions, fires, and many people dying. Today signs cry out "Don't break oil pipes" to discourage this activity which is spawned by the poverty facing most Nigerians. Human Immunodeficiency Virus (HIV) and Acquired Immune Deficiency Syndrome (AIDS) are also increasing rapidly and pose another very important threat to the people of Nigeria. Currently, more than 5 percent of the population is infected with this deadly disease.

Because of rampant corruption, most foreign investors have stayed away from Nigeria. There are almost no western corporations such as McDonald's, Kentucky Fried Chicken, Pizza Hut, or Burger King present in the country. Instead, local burger chains like Mr. Bigg's tempt hungry residents with hamburgers and other local food delights such as pepper soup, or the regionally popular jollof rice. The major exception, in the area of foreign investment, is in oil. Where petroleum wealth is involved, foreign presence is very common with international companies such as Shell, Texaco, and Exxon-Mobil being very actively involved in exploiting this resource. Nigeria is an oil-rich nation. Yet lines often stretch for blocks in front of gas stations that, ironically, do not have any gasoline to sell. Small vendors hawk "jerry cans" or plastic jugs of gasoline at a slightly higher price along the sides of roads. This oil shortage, in an oil-rich country, does not make sense at first glance, but a more detailed explanation will follow in Chapter 6.

Even with all of these problems, many Nigerians remain optimistic about their future and that of their country. A roadside sign in Port Harcourt states, "Bill Gates learned about computers when he was ten, your child can start earlier." Perhaps the candle of democracy, coupled with improved educational opportunities, will help to ignite more economic opportunities for the people of Nigeria. For this to happen, though, the rule of law rather than totalitarian despotism, will have to prevail if the country and its people are to enjoy a better future.

Despite these challenges and incongruities, the people of Nigeria provide warmth in their greetings and willingness to readily share with a smile their land and culture with visitors. The smile a visitor receives in Nigeria can mask other, deeper problems that will be investigated in this book. A smile can also project the optimism resulting from opportunities created by the new democratic constitution created and implemented in Nigeria in 1999. Hope and fear seem to grip the nation at the same time when considering its future. Yes, it is incongruous. There are so many apparent contradictions in Nigeria's past, present, and even in visions of the future. This is the Nigeria you will visit and explore in this book.

This is an example of an inselberg rock formation found in Central Nigeria. Inselbergs are created by the erosion action of water and wind over eons. They are usually composed of rock that is more resistant to erosion than the surrounding rock.

The Natural Environment

Nature, too, has presented Nigeria with incongruities. Natural agents have been both kind and cruel to the land and people who call Nigeria home. Dense, towering tropical rain forests, for example, suggest fertile soil; yet most tropical soils are notoriously infertile. The country's southern coastal area is drenched with up to 150 inches (3,810 millimeters) of precipitation each year; yet near-desert conditions occur in the northeast near Lake Chad. The lake itself is unique. Chad's basin drains into the interior, but is a freshwater body. Lakes with no outflow are generally saline (as in the Great Salt Lake in Utah). Lake Chad has no surface outflow, but scientists have determined that it is drained by subterranean (underground) flow. Deadly diseases from the natural environment also pose a constant threat to humans and animals alike. These are just some of the contradictory patterns you will learn about in this chapter.

THE LAND

Nigeria lacks the kinds of spectacular land features that are associated with many other areas of the African continent. The vast sea of shifting Saharan sand begins several hundred miles from the country's northern border. Just over 50 miles (80 kilometers) from its southeastern border, towering Mt. Cameroon rises 13,451 feet (5,000 meters) above the surrounding coastal plain. Nonetheless, Nigeria does have a number of distinctive physical regions.

To picture Nigeria's land features, think of a letter "Y" with its base to the south and its arms reaching northward. The letter, itself, represents the country's lowland regions. The low-lying coastal plain that drops gently toward the Gulf of Guinea forms the base of the "Y." Much of this region has been created by the alluvium (silt) deposited by the Niger River in its huge delta. Along the coast, sand and mud have created a variety of spits (a curved "hook" of land connected to the shore), bars, lagoons, beach ridges, and other coastal features. The stem of the "Y" is the broad floodplain of the Niger River downstream from its juncture with the Benue River. The arms of the "Y" represent the lowland plains of the Niger River to the west and Benue River to the east.

Nigeria also has three upland regions. North of the coastal plain and to the west of the "Y" is the relatively low Oyo-Yoruba upland. To the southeast of the right arm of the "Y" are the Adamawa highlands. Here, in eastern Nigeria and extending into neighboring Cameroon, several peaks exceed 6,000 feet (1,800 meters). Chappal Waddi, the highest point in Nigeria, rises to an elevation of 7,936 feet (2,419 meters). Between the raised arms of the "Y" rise the high plains of Hausaland, which rise to nearly 6000 feet (1,780 meters) on the Jos plateau. The Jos plateau features a number of extinct volcanic cones, some of which have lakes within their craters. Although elevations rarely reach more than one mile above sea level, the highlands do play a very important role in this tropical land. As a

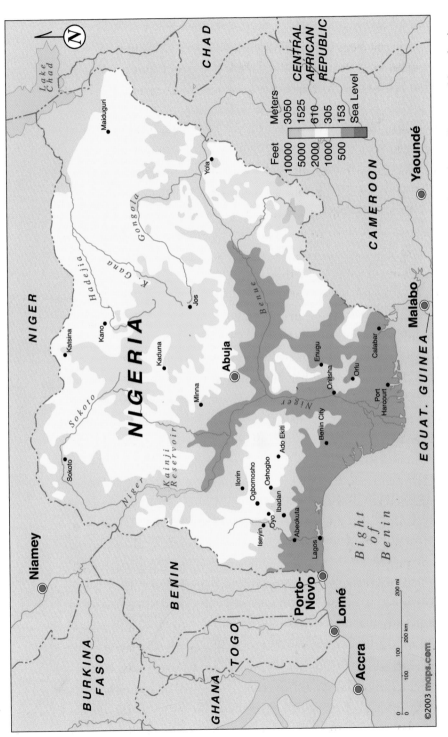

Nigeria is part of the area referred to as "Africa South of the Sahara." The shifting sands of the Sahara desert lie several hundred miles to the north of Nigeria's northern border. Its borders encompass both the rain-drenched southern coastal area and the near-desert conditions in the northeast.

general rule, temperatures drop by about 3.5° F (2° C) with each 1,000-foot (300-meter) increase in elevation. Uplands, therefore, are more comfortable and less prone to disease than the steaming tropical lowlands.

Finally, beyond the tips of both outstretched arms of the "Y" the land dips into basins. To the west, the lowland of the Niger River merges with the Sokoto basin formed by its tributary, the Kebbe-Sokota River. To the northeast, land drops gradually into the Chad basin that takes its name from the lake occupying its lowest point.

WEATHER AND CLIMATE

All of Nigeria falls within the tropics. Tropical locations are defined in various ways, perhaps the most common simply being any area "near the Equator." Many people define the region as including all of that part of Earth's surface lying between the tropics of Cancer (23 1/2° north latitude) and Capricorn (23 1/2° south latitude). With a latitudinal location between 4° and 14° north latitude, all of Nigeria conforms to this definition. What many people do not realize, however, is that "tropical" refers only to temperature. Climatologists are scientists who study Earth's long-term average weather conditions. They define a tropical location as being one in which the average temperature of the coldest month is above 65° F (18° C). Again, all of Nigeria conforms to the definition except for the highest mountain peaks.

Nigeria has three basic climate zones: wet tropical (tropical rain forest) near the coast; a seasonally wet and dry tropical (savanna) climate in the middle of the country; and a semiarid tropical (steppe) climate in the north. Going from south to north, conditions are wettest along the coast and become increasingly dry northward. Temperatures are hot throughout the country. The farther north one goes, however, the greater the daily, seasonal, and annual temperature variation or range.

Wet Tropical Climate

Southern Nigeria is constantly hot and humid. "Monotony" is the key word that describes the climate of this region. Temperatures and humidity remain fairly constant throughout the year. There is no "hot" or "wet" season, each day throughout the year being much like all others. In the coastal city of Lagos, in southwestern Nigeria, daytime high temperatures average around 95° F (35° C) throughout the year. Nighttime temperatures average around 70° F (21° C). As is typical of tropical locations, the annual average temperature is approximately 78–80° F (about 26° C). Rain falls almost daily and often in torrential amounts. The immediate coastal area receives 120 inches (3,048 millimeters) of precipitation each year and a few spots are drenched with up to 150 inches (3,810 millimeters). Imagine living in a place that receives 12 to 13 *feet* (3.8 meters) of rain a year! Nearly all rain occurs in short, but often very intense, thunderstorms.

Wet-and-Dry Tropical Climate

Seasonal wet-and-dry conditions prevail throughout a broad belt that includes roughly the middle half of Nigeria. This area has a climate marked by seasonal wet and dry conditions. During the high-sun ("summer") season of March to November, conditions are quite wet. Moisture-bearing winds blowing inland off the tropical waters of the Atlantic bring rain. Most areas receive between 30 and 60 inches (760–1,500 millimeters) of rainfall during the wet season. During low-sun ("winter") season, however, the wind direction reverses. A hot, dry, and often dusty wind called the *harmattan* blows southward from the Sahara Desert, bringing with it week after week of cloudless skies. Conditions become parched, much of the plant life becomes dormant or dies, and small streams and ponds become dry. Temperatures here experience greater extremes than in the wet tropics, exceeding 100° F (38° C) on hot days and dropping into the 60s° F (15°–20° C), or even lower in upland areas. Interestingly, the high-sun ("summer") season is not the warmest. Highest temperatures in this climatic zone occur just before and after the wet season. During the "spring" and "fall" seasons, the sky is relatively clear, allowing maximum sunlight and heating.

Semiarid Tropical Climate

Northern Nigeria falls within a narrow band of climate and vegetation called the *Sahel* which, translated from Arabic, means "coast" or "shore." The name comes from the region's location on the southern edge of the vast Sahara Desert, sometimes seen as a "sea" of sand and rock. Most of the Sahel receives 10–20 inches (250–500 millimeters) of precipitation annually, most of which falls during the high-sun ("summer") season. Temperatures here have a greater range, both daily and seasonally, than elsewhere in Nigeria. During the summer months, temperatures frequently soar well beyond 100° F (38° C). Winters, on the other hand, can get quite chilly. In northern Nigeria's largest city, Kano, temperatures have reached a sizzling 115° F (46° C) and dropped into the low 40s° F (6° C).

PLANT AND ANIMAL LIFE

Plant and animal life in Nigeria, as elsewhere, tends to correspond quite closely to climatic conditions. Because of the country's tropical conditions, moisture, rather than precipitation, is the key factor influencing plant life. Vegetation and water, in turn, are the key elements in creating wildlife habitat (the environmental conditions in which certain animals can live).

Natural vegetation shows sharp differences from south to north. Biogeographers recognize five general vegetation zones. Along the Atlantic coast and throughout much of the Niger Delta area, coastal mangrove and freshwater swamp prevails. Swamps are areas in which trees grow in standing water. Moving inland just a few miles, this zone gives way to dense

Harvesting timber from a Nigerian forest provides immediate economic benefits, but may severely affect the ecosystems of the region—its soil, plant, and animal life.

tropical rain forest, the dominant vegetation of the 'Wet Tropics.' The rain forest is home to hundreds of trees and other plant species. Some are commercially valuable, including hardwoods, such as mahogany, and the economically important oil palm. Most of the original tropical rain forest has been severely altered by human activity, including clearing of land for agricultural purposes. The rain forest teems with a huge variety of animal life. Large land animals include the forest elephant and chimpanzee. Crocodiles and hippopotamuses share the rivers with countless varieties of fish. Snakes, insects, and birds also are common to this ecosystem.

An area occupying roughly the central half of Nigeria is often referred to as the "Middle Belt." In this zone, the "wet-and-dry tropical climate" helps create a mixed woodland and tall grass savanna (tropical grassland) ecosystem. Here, trees such as the gnarled baobab, umbrella-shaped acacia, palms, and other species grow scattered among tall grasses. Species in this environment thrive during the wet season, but must be able to survive the several months-long period of drought as well. Fire has played a very important role in the creation of savanna landscapes. Each year, during the dry season, most of the savanna is deliberately burned over. Burning encourages the growth of fresh, tender grasses upon which livestock can graze. All plant life must be pyrophytic, or resistant to damage by fire. This is "big game" country. Lions, giraffes, hyenas, and several types of antelope are among the animals typical to this region.

Moving still farther northward, conditions begin to become increasingly arid and plant life more sparse. Tall grasses disappear, replaced by steppe (short) grasslands and a few smaller and more scattered trees. Grazing animals—both livestock and wild—share the steppe with various carnivores (meat eaters). Eventually, in the immediate area of the Lake Chad basin, desert conditions prevail.

SOILS

Roughly one-third of Nigeria is classified as being "arable" land, or land suited to agriculture of any kind. Nearly all of this land is used for grazing. Only about 3 percent of the country's total land area is in permanent crops. As mentioned previously, one reason so little land is farmed is that tropical soils are notoriously infertile. In the humid south, soils are either sandy or swampy, or, as in the forest belt, heavily leached or drained of nutrients. Northward, in the savanna region, soils are also leached and often turn to laterite, a brick-like soil that is difficult if not impossible to cultivate. Desert soils, where they exist, are fertile, but crop production depends upon available water for irrigation.

Fishermen cast their nets on Lekki Lagoon, near Lagos. This coastal city is the most populated and expensive area to live in Nigeria.

WATER FEATURES

Three features dominate Nigeria's hydrogeography: the Atlantic Ocean, the Niger River system, and Lake Chad. Marine resources play a relatively minor role in the country's economy. The sea gives the country a transportation window on the global ocean, and both Lagos and Port Harcourt are important ports. Marine conditions also play a vital role in the country's climate, particularly in the hot, humid, rainy south. Increasingly, the ocean floor has become an important source of Nigeria's chief natural resources, petroleum and natural gas.

The Niger River flows 2,600 miles (4,200 kilometers) across West Africa making it the country's third-longest stream. Although its headwaters lie far to the west, primarily in Guinea, the river's lower course and delta are in Nigeria. The Benue, flowing from the Adamawa highlands, is the major tributary. It joins the Niger at Lokoja, where its water doubles the volume of the longer stream. Upstream on the Niger, the Kainji dam and reservoir have been harnessed to produce hydroelectric energy. The Niger River delta is Africa's largest, occupying an area of about 14,000 square miles (36,000 square kilometers). It extends inland for nearly 150 miles (240 kilometers) and spreads for approximately 200 miles (320 kilometers) along the coast. Rather than being a single stream, at the head of the delta region, the river splits into many tributaries (channels).

A small strip of northeastern Nigeria faces the Lake Chad basin. During the drought of recent decades, this broad but very shallow freshwater lake has greatly shrunk in size.

NATURAL RESOURCES

Nigeria has a variety of valuable natural resources. They include soils for agriculture; water for domestic use, irrigation, industry, and hydroelectric energy production; tropical forests that produce hardwoods, palm oil, and other valuable products; and various minerals including tin, iron, lead, zinc, and columbite (an alloy used in the making of hardened steel). There is also industrial-grade limestone and deposits of coal.

Petroleum and natural gas, however, are the country's most important resources. Drilling and production began in 1958 in the Niger River delta region and offshore. Although the country's oil production amounts to only about 3 percent of the world's total, it accounts for 95 percent of Nigeria's exports. Clearly, oil is "king" in terms of its economic importance as is further discussed in chapters 4 and 8.

ENVIRONMENTAL HAZARDS AND ISSUES

Nigeria is relatively free of severe environmental hazards. Central and northern portions of the country suffer periodic drought conditions and flooding can occur in any location. As is true of any tropical location, various forms of animal life can pose a threat. One must constantly be on the watch for venomous snakes, crocodiles, lions, and other dangerous animals. The greatest threat, however, comes from tropical diseases, many of which are deadly. These include sleeping sickness, transmitted by the tse tse fly, which affects both humans and livestock; malaria, the world's most prevalent disease, which is transmitted by the *anopheles* mosquito; and river blindness, for which a black fly is the carrier.

The country also suffers from several environmental problems. Air, water, and soil alike are constantly being fouled by the petroleum industry operating with few environmental controls. In many places, soils are being lost or degraded by erosion, or simply becoming "worn out" from unwise farming practices. Forests throughout the country are being depleted at an alarming rate. In the northern third of Nigeria, the process of *desertification* is taking a severe toll on the land in many places. This environmental problem is the creation of desert conditions as a result of human activity. Over-grazing, farming in areas of marginal rainfall that occasionally leaves soil bare to erosion, and extensive cutting of trees for firewood and other purposes are the primary causes.

Over thousands of years, the inhabitants of what is now Nigeria have occupied this diverse and somewhat challenging natural landscape. Through time, people have culturally adapted to its various conditions; they have identified and used natural resources, often in different ways; and by their interactions with the environment, they have changed the natural landscape.

People of the earliest civilization in Nigeria, the Nok, made this sculpture. They lived from about 400 B.C. to 200 A.D., and must have been quite sophisticated to produce such craftsmanship.

3

Nigeria's
Early History

N igerians have a proverb for peace that states, "Two people quarreling do not share the same seat on a canoe." Yet Nigeria's past is filled with quarrels and infighting between its own people—different ethnic and religious groups. How has the country's history led to the society that exists today? With all of the turmoil experienced during the first few decades of Nigeria's history since independence, what historical elements of stability and chaos have been laid out in patterns that seem to foster disagreement and instability? These important questions lie behind our exploration of Nigeria's past and may lead to a better understanding of the present situation and the country's future.

NIGERIA'S EARLIEST PEOPLE

Compared to some areas of the world where humans have

existed for hundreds of thousands of years, Nigeria's past is not that ancient. Part of the reason for this is the difficulty that people had in reaching the region. The coastal area was inhospitable and very uncomfortable. It consisted of dense mangrove and woodland swamps teaming with tropical diseases. There was the ever-lurking danger of the tse tse fly, the bite from which could cause deadly sleeping sickness in people. It also can kill livestock, including horses that were a major early form of transportation. Malaria presented another threat. The Sahara Desert and Lake Chad discouraged travelers coming from the north and northeast.

Even the mighty Niger River discouraged sea access. Its water level shifts greatly from wet to dry season, resulting in changing sandbars and channel shifts that can cause constant peril to the river traveler. There are also dangerous rapids on the river. These factors and others helped to isolate Nigeria from outsiders and discouraged settlement for much of the region's early history. Some of these factors also served to block interactions between early kingdoms and ethnic groups.

The first known finding of people in what we now call Nigeria dates back about 10,000 years ago according to a skeleton found in the western part of the country. Various tools and other instruments, however, indicate that early human settlement existed even before that time. Agriculture started in the northern savanna region a few thousand years before the dawn of the Christian era and followed in southern Nigeria about 3,000 years ago.

The Nok culture is the first to be identified in the region. These people existed for about 600 years, from about 400 B.C. until the second century A.D. The Nok lived in the fertile lands in eastern Nigeria and to the area north and between the Niger and Benue rivers. The Nok were quite advanced as evident from the relics left from their ironwork and terracotta artwork. With the disappearance of the Nok, things seemed to fall silent for the next thousand years. Little information exists on this "silent millennium" in Nigeria's history.

Chief Ize of the Benin tribe can trace his people back to approximately 1400 A.D. when the Benin kingdom was at its most powerful.

EMERGENCE OF GREAT KINGDOMS

By the start of the second millennium, trade routes between areas in northern Nigeria and other areas of North Africa began to develop. Traders would bravely cross the Sahara to barter with the peoples living in what is now northern Nigeria. These northerners would then serve as a trade link between North Africans and other peoples further south. Beads, weapons, glassware, utensils, and cloth were important trade items. So were slaves, who were bought and sold by African peoples long before Europeans became involved in this tragic trade in human beings.

In the first half of the second millennium, various rich and powerful kingdoms emerged within the region. These early cultures formed the roots for some of the cultural groups existing in Nigeria today. Each of the kingdoms functioned as a separate state. They were independent from one another, each having its own political structure, cultural traditions, and social patterns. Primary among these independent kingdoms were the states of Yoruba, Hausa, Edo, Nupe, and Kanem.

Located west of the Niger River in southwest Nigeria is the area called Yorubaland. A mixture of people came to this area and mixed together to form the Yoruba culture region. Early in the second millennium, this mixture of people came together and formed a common language and culture that served as the roots of the modern Yoruba culture. Agricultural villages blended together during this time under a common chief who served as the leader of the region. The chief and his family evolved to become the monarchy of Yorubaland. The family claimed to have descended from Oduduwa, the creator of the earth and founder of the Yoruba's most important city, Ife.

Ife became both the seat of power and political influence for the Yoruba kingdom and also an important trade center. The king made money by taxing the trade. He also received offerings, as he was recognized as being the religious head. Over the next few hundred years the economic and political power center at Ife waned and the cities of Benin and Oyo rose to greater importance as trade centers. Oyo and Benin also had leaders with lineage drawing back to Oduduwa and the Ife dynasty. Oyo developed its own monarchy that was accompanied by a strong military.

Benin, the city, also became an important kingdom around the time of Columbus. Their king was called an *oba* and he ruled over lands far beyond just the city of Benin. Benin City is not to be confused with the modern country of Benin, which lies to the west of Nigeria. In the fifteenth century Benin had evolved into a great city with 100,000 people. Skilled workers dominated the economy and provided desirable goods for trading. Benin is world renowned for its bronze statues and artwork. Many of these statues were stolen and taken home by the British in the late nineteenth century. Thus, one will find that most of the best statues are in the British Museum in London. Very few of these prized pieces remain to be seen and appreciated in Benin city.

Trade centers located in the northern savanna regions of Nigeria were developed primarily by trade that came from across the Sahara Desert. Trade routes were developed and connected the Nigerian savanna to the Nile River valley, the Sudan, and the Mediterranean Sea. These same routes brought Islam, new knowledge, and technology to the region. The Hausa culture region began emerging around urban centers such as Kano, Gobir, Zaria, Nupe, and Katsina. These walled cities served as small kingdoms with leaders who were to have been descendents of Bayinjida, a legendary king. Kano is the oldest city in West Africa with a history that stretches back over a thousand years. Like Gobir and Katsina, Kano was a major center on trans-Saharan trading routes. These small kingdoms grew various agricultural products and produced both cloth and leather products.

The three small Hausa kingdoms were all quite equal in power, but faced a common threat in the powerful Songhai Empire that loomed to the west. Other immigrants also moved into Hausaland including cattle, sheep, and goat herders from the Senegal River area. These people brought their knowledge of raising domesticated animals to the region and soon became known to the Hausa as the Fulani. The Fulani, who were also Muslim, blended in easily with the Hausa people. Today, the two groups are the dominant cultures of northern Nigeria. They are virtually indistinguishable from each other and frequently are referred to collectively as the Hausa, or Hausa-Fulani, cultural group.

The earliest of the Nigerian kingdoms, Kanem and Borno,

were located near Lake Chad in northeast Nigeria. Like the other kingdoms in this northern region, trading was a major economic endeavor. The king of Kanem was called a *mai* and he adopted Islam as the religion of his kingdom around the end of the first millennium. Kanem had a strong army of slave soldiers and expanded its empire by taking control of Borno. The Kanem-Borno Empire fell apart in a civil war in the late fourteenth century when Borno again became an independent state. Borno was well known as a slave-trading kingdom and this trade brought great wealth.

Nupe was another smaller Muslim kingdom that developed in the fifteenth century. Many Fulani were also immigrants to this kingdom and were absorbed into the local culture. Like so many of the kingdoms, Nupe had its own separate language and customs and a king called an *etsu*. Because of their location in the Niger River valley north of the Benue River, they had more contact with western traders. This factor influenced the culture and made it different from neighboring cultural groups. This western impact still differentiates the Nupe people from others in northern Nigeria today.

The early history of the Ibo (Igbo) people is much less known than those described above. It is believed that the Ibo may have been mainly subsistence farmers who lived in smaller, scattered villages. Many anthropologists believe that many Ibo customs and traditions come from the small Nri kingdom that was located in Igboland.

EUROPEAN ARRIVAL AND IMPACT

The kingdom of Benin, which was located along the coast, was the first to have direct contact with Europeans. The Portuguese arrived and explored the West African coast as far as the Niger River delta in 1471. Portuguese traders soon followed these pioneer explorers. By 1481, they were engaged in active trade in spices and ivory with the kingdom of Benin. The Portuguese even supported Benin in wars with surrounding

Europeans first came to Africa as explorers and later as traders, missionaries, and colonial conquerors. Each role brought some benefit and tragedy to the Africans.

kingdoms. The new military technology received from the Europeans assisted Benin in battles with neighbors. Sadly, the Portuguese and Benin soon changed their trade from local natural resources and agricultural commodities to the more profitable slave trade. To the Benin's credit, they soon backed out of the European slave trade, even though the practice of slavery continued within Benin itself. This is only one example of Africans serving other Africans as slaves.

With the kingdom of Benin pulling out of the slave trade with Portugal, other kingdoms were very willing to move into this lucrative and inhumane practice. The coastal area in southwest Nigeria and of the country of Benin (not to be confused with the kingdom of Benin that was located near the modern-day city of Benin, Nigeria) came to be known as the "Slave Coast." Many of those enslaved by the Portuguese were forcibly moved from the Slave Coast to the New World and the Portuguese colony now known as Brazil. Although the Portuguese were the first to engage in slavery, soon other Europeans countries rushed in to buy and sell human slaves. Holland, England, France, and Spain also participated in the slave trade and used these people to further their economic interests. Most slaves performed labor in tropical and subtropical lands in the Americas where the European colonists were practicing plantation agriculture. In Africa, Africans would attack other Africans (often enemy tribes) to capture people and sell them into slavery with the Europeans. This inhumane trafficking imposed unbelievable hardship and misery to both those taken and the family and loved ones left behind.

Oyo and Aro kingdoms became leading slave-trading states in Nigeria. Each had elaborate networks to capture and sell slaves to the Europeans. Oyo would use its military might and western weapon technology to conquer other peoples and turn them over to slave buyers. This brought great wealth and technological power to Oyo which, in turn, was used to extend its reach even further. They were able to raid even more people and harvest even greater populations for the slave trade. Oyo fell apart in the Yoruba civil wars in the 1820s, while Aro, an Ibo state, continued its slave trade until much later.

Europeans developed a lucrative pattern of triangular trade that served the economic interests of the colonial European powers. Triangular trade worked as follows. The first leg of the triangle was slaves who were loaded on ships, often in ports such as Lagos, and taken to the New World and sold. Cotton, tobacco, sugar, and other raw materials were then shipped from the New World to the European colonial power, forming the second leg of the triangular trade. Then, to complete the triangle, manufactured goods, weapons, and other raw goods were shipped to Africa to trade for more slaves. The process was then repeated. The main beneficiary for all of this economic activity was, of course, the European nations.

England, Spain, France, Portugal, and the Netherlands sought and developed colonies in order to advance their efforts in the triangular trade. Even the Scandinavian countries of Denmark and Sweden briefly entered the slave trade. Some of the more active colonial powers, France, England, and Spain, thus expanded their colonial empires all around the world. This colony-building often caused these powerful countries to compete fiercely with each other, often resulting in wars. Several of these wars also spread to the colonies themselves, where much of the fighting took place and many local people were killed. By the eighteenth century, England had emerged as the leading trans-Atlantic slave-trading nation, followed by Portugal and France. By 1712, the British had a virtual monopoly over Africa's West Coast slave trade, including coastal Nigeria.

For Africans, including Nigerians, this time period was truly a nightmare. Millions of African people were sold into slavery; African chiefs and other people seeking to profit from trade in human beings captured and sold the slaves to the Europeans. Because of the oppressive heat and humidity, diseases, and other factors, Europeans themselves rarely if ever went on shore. The slaves were loaded onto the ships, their life and destiny having been traded for a few European trinkets; many of the slaves died in transit; conditions on the slave ships were inhumane. People were packed together in spaces so tiny they could barely lie down without touching someone else. Food and water were scarce, the stench was overwhelming, and diseases killed many. People were treated as a commodity, rather than as human beings. Ironically, some historians believe that even more Europeans than slaves died in transit. They, after all, were unaccustomed to the tropical climatic conditions and had no resistance to African diseases.

Nigeria suffered immensely from the slave trade. It is estimated that as many as 3.5 million Nigerians were sold into slavery during the 400-year trading period. Yoruba and Ebo people were most frequently sold and enslaved, but significant

Slave capturing and trading was first common among African tribes and was quickly adopted by European and Western traders. The plentiful source of cheap labor proved too lucrative for them to pass up.

numbers of Hausa and other ethnic groups also suffered at the hands of this despicable practice. In addition, the practice caused great divisions between different Nigerian cultural groups. Intertribal warfare became increasingly common, as neighboring groups fought to gain captives who, in turn, were sold into slavery. Mistrust of the Europeans also was heightened because of the slave trade and the other corrupt practices with which they had become associated. Thus the slave trade in Nigeria not only destroyed families, but also damaged cultures, and intercultural relations.

The British actually ended their involvement in the slave trade in 1807 when Parliament made it illegal for British citizens to own slaves. Even with this law, the British colonial presence in Nigeria remained stronger, although no longer involved in trading in slaves. The slave trade with other Europeans was finally abolished in 1870. Sadly, according to the United Nations, some slave trade continues in Africa even today.

When slave trade finally ended in Nigeria in the late nineteenth century, the ethnic groups of the region were very divided. Hatred existed between many because of the effects of the slave trade and wars between various groups. To say the region was politically disrupted would be an understatement. While the south had gone through the horror and disruption of slavery and the slave trade, the north had been conducting an active trans-Saharan trade. In the nineteenth century, the Fulani rebelled in a religious war called a *jihad* and seized control of the Hausa kingdoms in an effort to advance their Islamic faith. They established a caliphate in the city of Sokoto and sought to bring back traditional Islamic religious values.

Regional differences and disharmony were very strong at the start of the twentieth century. The following chapter provides insights into British involvement in Nigeria and how, ultimately, the country achieved independence.

Over a hundred years of the devastating slave trade caused serious intertribal conflicts and warfare. The resulting power vacuum was filled by European countries that colonized almost all of Africa.

4

British Nigeria and Independence

S ince trading in slaves had been banned by British Parliament in 1807, British traders now embarked on different and more palatable trade. Palm oil became a very important export for the British in Nigeria. The Royal Niger Company and other British trading companies were set up to operate in Nigeria. The Royal Niger Company, headed by George Goldie, had firmly established itself in the Niger River basin by the 1880s. With British financial interests solidly rooted in Nigeria, France, Germany, and other European colonial powers were kept away from the region. The groundwork had been laid for British territorial and political claims on Nigeria.

GROWING BRITISH INFLUENCE

British missionaries also worked to advance Christianity in Nigeria. Beginning in the mid-nineteenth century, missionaries brought the

Anglican, Catholic, and various Protestant denominations to the region. At the same time, the British were starting to develop political control over strategic areas in Nigeria. Treaties were signed with some groups, including the Sokoto kingdom in the north. In the coastal region, the British established the Lagos Colony in 1861. By the 1890s, the Royal Niger Company controlled the Niger River delta. Other coastal lands were designated as a British Protectorate. The status of a protectorate is lower than that of a colony like Lagos. But it nonetheless shows the increasing political control the British were exercising in the region. By the start of the twentieth century, the British grip on the area now known as Nigeria was tightening.

In 1897, Lord Frederick Lugard was appointed by the British to be the commissioner of northern Nigeria. A strong leader with a thick droopy mustache, his entry brought huge changes to Nigeria. In reality, Lugard was sent by the British to take over for the Royal Niger Company, whose services were terminated in 1899, and to establish control over the entire region of Nigeria. He was a strong leader and very adept at his task. When diplomacy failed, he would conquer militarily with a great show of force. This show of strength was used to eliminate resistance by others who had heard of his lopsided victories. After victory, Lugard would rule the newly conquered area through the ruler who had been in place before. Thus, he set them up as puppet rulers who were quick to jump into action on his behalf when requested to do so. Lugard left Nigeria in 1903, but he had started the process of putting all of Nigeria into British hands. Others followed his work and consolidated southern Nigeria into a protectorate by 1906.

Lugard returned to Nigeria in 1912. His task this time was to unite the Northern and Southern Protectorates into one political entity. This was accomplished by 1914. Lugard and the British still ruled indirectly through their local puppet leaders, but he formed a Nigerian council that included the various cultural groups represented. Even though all of Nigeria was brought together in the early twentieth century, little meaningful contact took place between the regions. Differences in environment, history, and culture between the north and south were enormous. These differences continue to plague the country even today. Lugard left Nigeria again in 1918. Because of his basic unifying work in the country, he is considered to be a key figure in the creation of the entity we now refer to as Nigeria.

The governor general who followed Lugard allowed more direct Nigerian involvement in political decision making. This allowed Nigerian political parties to form and also ignited a Nigerian nationalist spirit. This spirit initially called for greater Nigerian involvement in the political processes. This was important as the south was increasingly showing the influences of the British in cultural patterns and language, while the north was against these western influences. Nevertheless, nationalism grew in both regions during the time between World Wars I and II. This nationalism resulted in the loud cry for self-government. Religion also was impacted by the new nationalism. Christianity started to take on definite Nigerian characteristics and, in some cases, was becoming independent from western denominations.

The political independence spirit moved forward with political parties such as the Lagos-based Nigerian National Democratic Party (NNDP) led by Herbert Macauley, a man who is known as the Father of Nigerian nationalism. He owned the Lagos newspaper and used it as a forum for Nigerian nationalism. He and his NNDP party, and its successor the National Youth Movement (NYM), argued for greater Nigerian participation in the government as civil servants. Macauley also pushed for better education for the Nigerian people. Although political parties in the 1920s and 1930s tended to be regional and often culture based, these early efforts by Macauley helped to develop and extend the spirit of Nigerian nationalism.

During World War II, Nigeria fought meritoriously for the Allies in Ethiopia, Burma, Palestine, and other locations. These hearty efforts told the British that Nigeria's self-rule may need to be addressed in the near future. The major problem with independence was the immense regional cultural fragmentation that continued to exist in the country after World War II. Each major ethnic group—the Hausa, Yoruba, and Ibo—had their own political party. In the region where the ethnic group existed, their party was almost totally dominant. In other cultural regions, though, the party would get almost no support. Additionally, population numbers favored the Islamic north, but the Muslims feared that the more highly educated people in the south would prevail in the democratic processes.

What was the British answer? After wrestling with this continuing division, the British decided to develop a constitution that would reflect the differences in the three major cultural regions. There were many failed attempts to create a constitution before independence in 1960, simply because of the regional differences. Thus, the British finally divided the country into three regions, the Hausa north, the Yoruba southwest, and the Ibo southeast. Each was to govern in its own region with its own courts and civil service. At the national level the problem of division still existed. Each group feared that the others might prevail and set the tone for the entire new country of Nigeria after independence. With the discovery of oil and the exports that followed, the group holding political power would also decide what would be done with tax revenues from this new and valuable resource. Power in Lagos under the new constitution of an independent Nigeria would be very important.

INDEPENDENT NIGERIA

On October 1, 1960, Nigeria became an independent nation and a member of the United Nations. A huge celebration at the stadium in Lagos marked independence. Three years later, in 1963, Nigeria became a member of the British Commonwealth. The country finally had become master of its own destiny. However, like the proverb about people quarreling in the canoe, there were still the three major ethnic groups quarreling among themselves. Clearly, there were huge differences regarding national governance. The British had called a diverse group of Nigerians together to write the new constitution, but the many and complex issues relating to ethnic regional divisions remained a huge obstacle. As an example, when the new Nigerian capital was established in Lagos, the heart of the Yoruba region, other regions were alarmed. They believed (and correctly so) that this move would shift the balance of power to the Yoruba.

After independence, the membership of the new House of Representatives favored the Hausa region. This northern, Islamic group had the largest population in the country. The Hausa political candidates gained 174 of the 312 seats, a majority, in the House and their political party, the Northern People's Congress (NPC) had only run candidates for office in the Hausa North. No one representing the NPC ran for the House in other regions. The ethnic link to political parties also remained very strong in other regions of the country. The 44 members of the Senate were selected by the regional legislatures.

With this majority, the British asked the leader of the NPC party to form a government. Sir Abubakar Tafawa Balewa of the NPC was selected as the prime minister, and Nnamdi Azikiwe was appointed governor general. Azikewe had been a long-time advocate for Nigerian unity and Balewa was also a respected political moderate.

A HOUSE DIVIDED

After independence, new states were carved out of the regions of Nigeria. This was done to reflect the self-determination desires of other smaller ethnic groups. The linking of political realms with ethnic groups (often involving religious differences, as well) allowed for the differences existing between these various groups. But a national identity for all of Nigeria would be much more difficult to forge. Political infighting dominated the early 1960s. The ethnic political parties occasionally created uneasy coalitions, but these would usually fall apart in squabbles at the national level. The disintegration of the Yoruba's political party also brought more instability to the political processes in Lagos.

Since the House of Representatives was based on population, southerners held high hopes that the 1963 census would give them a majority in the body over the Hausa north. With the decline of the Yoruba parties, a southern alliance was developed to counter the larger population in the north. A scandal erupted with the release of the census results that seemed to greatly inflate the population—by more than 20 million!

The ruling coalition started unraveling in the mid-1960s when corruption and mistrust between the political elements increased to untenable levels. The elections of 1964 and 1965 were very corrupt and many citizens boycotted the elections. Protests erupted in the west and violence followed, resulting in the death of thousands of people. This was followed in January, 1966, by a military coup led mainly by General Ironsi and other Ibo officers who assassinated Prime Minister Balewa and other political and military leaders. The coup caused more division and unrest. The infighting became even more intense until it finally erupted into a virtual war with troops from different regions fighting each other for control of the government. Muslim officers overthrew the Ibo military government in July 1966 and assassinated General Ironsi. However, instead of raising a Muslim officer as leader, they selected Yakubu Gowan, a moderate young Christian officer, known as Jack Gowan, to lead Nigeria.

The Ibo were resentful over the Muslim coup. They also detested the leadership of Gowan and, hence, did not recognize his government. At the same time, thousands of Ibo were being killed in the north. Lieutenant Colonel Chukwuemeka Odumegwu Ojukwu, an Ibo, could not accept the horror of the ongoing conflict. In 1967, he declared independence from Nigeria and Gowan's government. Ojukwo then created a new country called Biafra, which was a slice taken from eastern Nigeria. This started a civil war between Nigeria and the rogue

The Ibo people in eastern Nigeria rebelled against the new Muslim federal government in the late 1960s and fought the Biafran War to win independence for a separate, ill-fated country called Biafra.

Ibo region of Biafra. Some countries recognized Biafra as an independent state and sent aid. Others supported Nigeria during the war. In the end, it is estimated that as many as two million people died in the three-year war. Many were killed in the fighting, but hundreds of thousands of people died of starvation and disease. By the end of 1970, Biafra no longer existed and Nigeria was once again whole—but with a broken soul.

PETROLEUM AND POLITICS

Fortunately the oil boom of the early 1970s helped Nigeria quickly put the civil war behind them. Oil prices spiraled upward and brought huge new revenues to Nigeria. The spike in world oil prices inspired Nigeria to import expensive goods and services from abroad. Oil became the star of Nigeria's economy in the early 1970s, a position the resource continues to hold today. However, when oil prices stabilized in the mid-1970s, crime and corruption became increasingly rampant in the country, and inflation became a huge problem. In addition, droughts in the north eroded agricultural production. Nigeria was in trouble.

The Gowan regime, for a number of reasons, was also falling out of favor with the population. First among them was Jack Gowan's promise to restore civilian rule by the mid-1970s. This combined with the blatant crime, corruption, and economic problems led to Gowan being overthrown in a military coup led by General Murtala Mohammed in 1975. This new military government attempted to clean up the corrupt government and military.

In 1976 Mohammed was killed in another coup attempt, but his regime stayed in power. Selected to lead was General Olusegun Obasanjo, a Yoruba. One of his main goals was to return Nigeria to civilian rule as quickly as possible. The Constitution of 1979 was drafted by the Obasanjo government and implemented in the same year. This was the start of the Second Republic. Civilian rule had finally returned to Nigeria after nearly 14 years of military rule. Shehu Shagari was elected as president.

The Shagari government lasted less than four years. It wildly overspent its budgets, a condition at least partially resulting from a sharp decline in the price of oil. Another military coup took place on New Years Eve in 1983 and General Mohammed Bahari was installed as president. He, in turn, was removed by General Babangida in another military coup in 1985. Thus, the pattern of struggle between military and civilian rule had become very much Nigeria's path by the end of the 1980s.

A breakthrough occurred in the elections of 1993 when, for the first time ever, people voted across ethnic lines. Sadly, Babangida annulled the election results. This new voting development, however, brought promise for a Nigerian national identity that could exist beyond a person's own ethnic group. Under pressure, Babangida appointed a civilian president, Ernest Shonekan, in August of 1993, but this government only lasted until November. It was replaced peacefully by the military government of Sani Abacha who died of a heart attack in 1998. Abacha's successor, General Abdulsalan Abubakar, was committed to restoring civilian rule as soon as possible. This was accomplished with the Constitution of 1999 and the election of Olusegun Obasanjo as president. This is the same man who was the leader of the military government in the late 1970s. The presidency of Obasanjo marked the beginning of Nigeria's Third Republic.

Nigeria's past has been filled with ethnic and religious strife. It also has a political heritage that is marked with conflict and a struggle between military and civilian rule. Today, Nigeria is in the midst of its strongest civilian rule since independence. For the first time in history, many people are viewing themselves as "Nigerians" as well as Hausa, Ibo, Yoruba, or some other ethnic group. Even with the new high hopes resulting from the Constitution of 1999, the seams of Nigerian society continue to be torn and frayed on a regular basis. Religious splits and ethnic divisions can still quickly ignite into flames of violence and death.

Many observers believe that Nigeria today is really two countries instead of one—the Muslim north and the Christian south. It is a country forced together by the British who imposed political rule over a land sharply divided in terms of its physical environment, natural resources, people, and ways of life. Much like the proverb about the two people in a canoe, only time will show whether these uncomfortable neighbors can share the same country we know as Nigeria.

Religious conflict in Nigeria has increased rather than diminished in recent years. In 2002, a controversial newspaper article about the Miss World beauty pageant, which was being hosted by Nigeria, caused mass rioting and burning of buildings.

5

People and Religion

"You are welcome." This traditional Nigerian greeting is quickly and repeatedly extended to visitors. It is a warm greeting from the people of this country who are very courteous and who provide generous hospitality even with limited resources. It is also a part of the puzzle of how Nigeria is contradictory, or incongruent. Nigeria's incongruence begins and ends with its people. The country's human diversity is much like a stew of many different ingredients, all simmering together in one pot. However, unlike most well-planned stews, this pot hold ingredients that sometimes don't taste very good when put together. This describes the mix of people living in Nigeria today.

Nigerians are a mix of two major and many minor religions, and the country's people represent various ethnic groups with long histories of animosity, resulting in resentful memories of repeated terror and tragedy. These divisions can be illustrated by a tragic event that occurred in November 2002. The Miss World Pageant was to be held in Nigeria's capital city of Abuja. A young Christian female journalist for *This Day*, a local newspaper in the city of Kaduna, wrote an article in favor of the pageant in which she suggested that even the prophet Muhammad would have favored the event. This article angered many Muslims. In Kaduna, they were incited to burn the offices of *This Day*, many cars, and even Christian churches. They also harassed and killed Christians. Christians retaliated by burning mosques and persecuting Muslims. The crises quickly escalated and moved on to the capital city of Abuja, where the pageant contestants were being held in the Nicon Hilton Hotel. Before the violence had subsided, thousands of people were injured and hundreds killed in the religious fighting that took place. The pageant was then moved to London and Nigeria was humiliated on the world stage because of this tragic incident. Millions of dollars in potential tourist revenue also were lost. The young woman journalist who wrote the article was forced to flee Nigeria for her safety.

The same type of tragedy happened after the September 11, 2001, attacks on U.S. sites, the twin towers of the World Trade Center and the Pentagon. Hundreds of innocent victims were killed in religious violence between Muslims and Christians in northern Nigeria. To understand the bitterness and potential of the country's cultural stew, this chapter and the next investigate both the religious and other cultural elements that shape the human landscape today. While the stew may sometimes be bitter, progress has been made toward developing tolerance and sweetening the pot in this culturally diverse country.

NIGERIA'S HUMAN MOSAIC

What are the characteristics of Nigeria's people? According to estimates, the population is approximately 130 million, ranking the country ninth among nations. There are more people in Nigeria than in the rest of West Africa combined. Not only does the country have a huge number of people, the population continues to grow at an alarming 2.5 percent per year (the world average is 1.3 percent). Nigeria is a country with a booming population. On the average, a woman will give birth to five or six children, a factor that contributes to this rapidly increasing population. With the depressed living conditions facing most Nigerians, life expectancy for both men and women is only 52 years. This average life span is far below the world average 67-year life span, and 76-year span in the world's developed countries.

HIV-AIDS is a growing menace in Nigeria as it is throughout much of Africa south of the Sahara. It is estimated that over 5 percent of the population is now infected with this often deadly disease, and the number is increasing at an alarming rate. This startling factor could unfortunately reduce the rate of population increase, as efforts to address the problem have had little success.

One way to sharply reduce population growth is to improve the level of educational attainment and literacy among women. Presently, about 67 percent of Nigeria's males are literate, but only 47 percent of females can read and write. This leaves the country with an overall literacy rate of only 57 percent. Research consistently shows that in countries where female literacy is increased, a sharp decline in the birthrate also is experienced. In Nigeria, there is often a conflict between education and population growth. In many families, children must work to help support their family and therefore cannot attend school. The cycle of illiteracy, poverty, and large families, thus continues.

CITIES IN NIGERIA

Major cities in Nigeria reflect the culture of the region in which they are located. Major cities include Lagos, Port Harcourt, Kano, and Abuja, the capital. Lagos is located in the Yoruba region, Port Harcourt in the Ibo region, and Kano in the Hausa region. Abuja is situated in the center of these three major cultural regions and was created in this location in an effort to try to unify the factionalism that exists in Nigeria and has long divided the country.

Lagos is a huge, violent, polluted and crime-plagued city with over 13 million people. Most of the city rests on four islands that are connected with too few bridges. Highways and streets are choked with cars, buses, trucks, vans, and street vendors all of which severely hamper the flow of traffic. With its rapid growth rate, Lagos will most likely be one of the ten largest cities in the world by 2025.

As Nigeria's major population center, Lagos serves as the main transportation hub for international and domestic air service and its port is a major trading point for the country. Lagos was the capital of Nigeria until 1991, but most of the foreign embassies and governmental agency headquarters have now moved their offices to the new capital in Abuja. The National Museum is still in Lagos and it holds pieces of the outstanding ivory and bronze sculpture from Benin.

Port Harcourt, a major port city with a population of over one million, is located in the Ibo cultural region. It is in the heart of Nigeria's important oil region and serves as home to some of the country's main oil refineries. The eastern railroad also ends in Port Harcourt, so the city helps to move products into and out of the interior. The city also has an international airport, but with limited connections to other countries.

Kano is located in the Hausa cultural region and is a large city with over three million people. Kano is West Africa's oldest city, dating back more than 1,000 years to 998 when it was first settled. It was an early trading city heavily involved in the trans-Saharan movement of goods. Islam came to Kano in the 1500s and the city continues to serve as a religious center in the Hausa region. The "Old City" of Kano is a draw for tourists. Other attractions are the central mosque and the Emir's Palace, in which an emir continues to live.

A train station also serves as a marketplace in Lagos, Nigeria. Unconventional, independent business practices illustrate the attempt to rebuild the collapsed economy caused by years of military rule.

Kano is also a major agricultural, trading, and industrial center. Cotton is grown and made into textiles. Cattle are raised for food, shoes, and other leather goods. Other important products are peanuts, peanut products, and soap.

Abuja is a planned national capital city that is located in the middle of the three major cultural regions. With Abuja, political leaders also hoped to open up the interior of Nigeria to more settlement. The city is designated formally as the

Federal Capital Territory for Nigeria, much like the District of Columbia in the United States. Abuja holds the three national branches of government and their related offices. This includes buildings such as the National Assembly, the presidential complex, and the Supreme Court. The National Assembly is in a beautiful setting with the impressive backdrop of Aso Rock that stands majestically behind the building.

Abuja was originally planned to be a city of no more than 3.1 million and a world showcase for Nigeria. However, a problem now facing the capital is the rapid population growth due to people migrating into the city. This is causing it to become bloated well beyond the original plans. In fact, a September 2002 article in *This Day*, a major Lagos newspaper, indicated that Abuja is now home to more than four million people. Even with the growth, a visitor will be impressed with the city's architecture of the mosque and government buildings. Nearby Zuma Rock is also a draw for visitors.

The cities just described, except Abuja, are situated in differing cultural regions. They are frequently featured in the news when ethnic or religious strife breaks out, often with violence and death. Each city and region has a flavor different from the other, but each also contributes to the distinctive cultural landscape of this incongruent country.

Nigeria's religious, ethnic, and regional diversity has been a source of great division and unrest. These differences have made it more difficult to create a Nigerian national identity, as the cultural identity—particularly the religious divisions—has been foremost in the minds of Nigerians. Some needed changes are now taking place in this arena, but the divisions still occasionally taint the stew.

RELIGION IN NIGERIA

As noted previously, there are two primary religions in Nigeria, Christianity and Islam. Both are practiced by roughly half of the population, with Christianity being prevalent in the south and Islam in the north. Indigenous religions, or animist beliefs, are practiced by less than 10 percent of the population, primarily by some Ibo and Yoruba in the south. Animism believes that there is a force or spirit within all things, whether they are real or imagined.

More Nigerians practice Islam than any other religion. Half of the population (50 percent) is Muslim and they comprise a vast majority of the population in the north. Some Yoruba and almost all Hausa and Fulani are Muslim. Islam affects nearly every aspect of life in the north and visitors easily notice its effects. During recent years, the Muslims have become increasingly more fundamentalist in their beliefs and practices. One example is the return and implementation of traditional *Sharia* Islamic law in many northern states since 1999 when military rule ended.

Sharia law is drawn from the *Koran* and holds practitioners strictly to the teachings contained in Islam's most holy book. This code of law requires specific, harsh punishments for specific offenses, regardless of circumstances. For example, the hands of a cow thief have been cut off and young Nigerian youth have been whipped for engaging in sex before marriage. Today, courts to uphold Sharia law exist in 12 states in northern Nigeria. Sharia causes great problems for Christians in the region who do not feel that they are treated equitably by the Islamic courts. Frequently the national government has been called in to question and often overturn the decisions of the Sharia courts. For example, in 2002, a woman was to be stoned to death for committing adultery. The Nigerian national government overturned this decision and the ruling by the local Sharia court. Thus, Sharia law frequently brings the national government into conflict with the Muslim population as the punishments can be seen as inequitable, extreme, or unfair.

The conflict between Sharia law and the constitution of Nigeria is a great potential source of conflict. The Nigerian

This 35-year-old Nigerian woman, Safiya Husaini, was sentenced to death by stoning in an Islamic court in northern Nigeria. Husaini is divorced and was sentenced to death for adultery after bearing this child out of wedlock. Here she is shown with 10-month-old Adama in her home in Sokoto, northern Nigeria. Her case became a focal point for human activists around the world.

Constitution states that people are Nigerian citizens first. Their religion, whether it be Christian or Muslim, comes second to national citizenship. However many Muslims believe that Sharia law should not be less important than the constitution. With the introduction of Sharia law after 1999, conflicts between it and the constitution and national government have increased greatly. Christians in the Muslim north believe that Sharia law discriminates against them. This battle promises to continue for the foreseeable future.

Soon after Muhammad's lifetime (570–632 A.D.), Islam spread across much of North Africa including the area of present-day northern Nigeria. At the same time the Hausa, Fulani, and Kanuri peoples moved into what is now northern Nigeria. Nearby rulers of Songhai, located in what today is Mali, controlled the largest empire in West Africa. They also adopted Islam from Arab traders and extended the Songhai Empire into the Nigerian region that was then occupied by the Hausa. The city of Kano became a great center for Islam in the region. All of these historical events planted the seeds of Islam deep into the history and culture of northern Nigeria by the beginning of the sixteenth century.

Not surprisingly, the Hausa language in the north adopted many Arabic words that are still present in the language today. Other effects of Islam on northern Nigeria include closer relationships between religion and the governments in the area. Since Muhammad was also a theocratic government leader—a leader believed to be divinely guided—the relationship between government and Islam has usually been close. This is very different from Western nations where there is usually a separation of church and state. The close relationship existing between government and Islam has usually restricted, or even prohibited, religious freedom. Additionally, government is often used as a tool of religion to subjugate individuals under the combined power of the two institutions of government and religion.

The first instance of Sharia law in Nigeria was in the early nineteenth century. This accompanied the development of a virtual empire called an Islamic caliphate in the north of Nigeria and adjacent lands. This caliphate lasted for over 100 years, until 1903, when the British, led by Lord Frederick Lugard's West African Frontier Force, killed the caliph and seized the cities of Kano and Sokoto. Lugard then created the Protectorate of Northern Nigeria and the British appointed the leader to the region who was called a sultan. During the twentieth century, under British rule, the notion of a Nigerian entity or state was nurtured. This meant that Islam was subjugated to the central British authority and that the rules of the culture and Sharia were disestablished.

Today, a visitor to the north will see all elements of Islam present. The traditional clothing, girls taught by women, the call to prayer, modern mosques, and Arabic influences on language are all seen in everyday life. Muslims are expected to abide by the Five Pillars of Islam, which include declaring their faith, daily prayers, paying the *zakat* tax, fasting during Ramadan, and making a pilgrimage to Mecca at least once in their lifetime. Nigerians who have made the pilgrimage to Mecca are called *al-Hajj*. Call to prayer takes place five times a day by music played over loudspeakers. This singing pervades the cities in the north at the designated times. Muslims prepare for prayer and will excuse themselves from meetings or work to pray on their knees, usually in private or with other Muslims. On Fridays, their holy day, most Muslims will go to their mosque to pray.

Many Nigerians died in New York City in the World Trade Center tragedy and following the September 11, 2001 attack, many others also died in northern Nigeria as a result of related rioting. Today, a visitor will see cars with stickers and pictures portraying Osama bin Laden as a hero. Inasmuch as many of their fellow citizens died as a result of these tragic events, such behavior, too, seems strange.

With the end of the military rule in 1999, the tension between Islam and the central government has continued. A particularly strong irritant is the reintroduction and implementation of traditional Islamic values and structures such as Sharia law. Can the country afford this incongruence with the national government and constitution? Can the country afford and survive the religious divisions existing in Nigeria? These and other questions are things to watch for as Nigeria moves forward in the third millennium.

The other major religion in Nigeria is Christianity, which is practiced by 40 percent of the people. This is not one Christian faith or denomination but a wide variety of Christian groups that range from small neighborhood congregations that look like small stores, to large churches with thousands of members. Traditional Christian church denominations such as Methodist, Roman Catholic, Assembly of God, Baptist, Jehovah's Witness, and Lutheran are present. So is the British Anglican Church and thousands of small independent ministries that sprout like dandelions in Nigeria's southern cities.

Traveling the roads of southern Nigeria presents a feast of local churches with names that tantalize the imagination. For example, there is the Christ Embassy, Deeper Life Bible Church, Celestial Church of Christ, Pentecostal Power and Fire Ministries, Victorious Life Church, Bluebell Harvest Church, Heroes of Faith Ministries, Champion Faith Assembly, and the Inheritance of Mercy Mission, to name but a few. As many as 50 of these small churches may appear within a single mile, when traveling though a city. Certainly there exists an abundance of choices when it comes to selecting a Christian faith in southern Nigeria today. The greatest variety is found in Ibo communities in the southeast, as the Ibo have adopted Christianity to a greater extent than other major ethnic groups. As is true in the West, visiting a Christian church on a holiday such as Easter Sunday is an important event for Nigerians. Dress may take on wild and vivid colors like bright orange,

Nigerian Christians typically spend New Year's Eve in church joyously praying for their families. The exuberant native culture has put its own mark on traditional, staid Christianity.

yellow, and green. Some women wear traditional head wrappings that are truly stunning with a rainbow of bright colors. Others wear hats that appear very western in their style and may have come from the styles set in Paris or New York.

Christian services may possess traditional religious practices of the denomination, but they also incorporate the vibrant Nigerian elements of song and dance. The offering alone can be a wonderful rhythm-filled dancing parade of the parishioners to an offering collection point in the front of the church. The collection alone can take over an hour as the music and dancing spirit takes over the service. Other aspects of traditional religions, such as respect for ancestors and even magic, are often incorporated into Christianity.

Christianity came to Nigeria with colonialism in the late 1800s, when many missionaries arrived hoping to gain converts to their religion. In the nineteenth century, most westerners considered Africans to be inferior. The often greatly exaggerated missionary reports of the era described Africa as a desolate, savage, primitive, crime-filled, wretched, and immoral land. The crusaders believed that their mission was to save these people from themselves and proceeded to carry their messages forward. Some of the early Protestant missionaries were freed slaves who had returned to Liberia or Sierra Leone.

While the missionaries' colonial view of native Nigerians may have been biased, the missionaries actually made many contributions to African societies. For example, they helped to develop written languages for many of the regional languages. English was taught to the locals and the missionaries also helped with education, medicine, agriculture, and architecture in addition to their religious teachings.

Religion has flavored some of the ingredients for the people of Nigeria. The next chapter will add a variety of cultural groups to this mix.

Some Yoruba people display their traditional clothing. The other two major ethnic groups are the Ibo and Hausa-Fulani. Such diversity is, both, one of Nigeria's greatest assets and hindrances.

6

Nigeria's Cultural Groups

igeria is rich in cultural diversity with over 250 ethnic groups. As mentioned before, three groups stand out as being the country's largest and most influential. The first of these groups is the Yoruba, who are located mostly in the southwestern part of the country around Lagos. The second is the Hausa, who are located in the north. The third large ethnic group is the Ibo, who are dominant in the southeast. Other ethnic groups abound in Nigeria, but are much smaller and less influential than the three primary groups. Some of the other ethnic groups are the Edo located in the west, the Ibibio and Ijaw located in the east, and the Fulani, Kanuri, Nupe, and Tiv located mainly in the North.

Because of the diverse cultures, varieties in language also are great. In fact, nearly 250 distinctly different linguistic groups are

PERCENTAGE OF POPULATION
BY ETHNIC GROUP

ETHNIC GROUP	NUMBER	PERCENTAGE
Hausa-Fulani	37,681,123	29%
Yoruba	27,286,331	21%
Ibo (Igbo)	23,388,283	18%
Ijaw	12,993,491	10%
Kanuri	5,197,396	4%
Ibibio	4,547,722	3.5%
Tiv	3,248,373	2.5%
Other	15,592,189	12%

*Estimates based on *2002 CIA World Factbook* data

found within the country. Only a few people speak the minor languages, but millions speak the main languages which are Hausa, Ibo, and Yoruba. With the strong influence left by the British, English is the true national language and serves as the official language that is used by government and business.

YORUBA

The Yoruba peoples are the largest ethnic group in West Africa. Over 20 million people speak the Yoruba language today. Various theories exist as to where the Yoruba people got their start. Legend holds that they are from Ile Ife, a town in Yorubaland where a mythical king named Oranyan is supposedly buried. Others believe that the Yoruba came from

Egypt or Saudi Arabia and migrated to Ile Ife. The group unified with a kingdom in the eighteenth century, but was later divided into four states. Other cities like Benin and Oyo developed separate Yoruba groupings. More divisions took place when the British arrived and seized control of Yoruba-land. Many smaller sects developed with their own language and cultural variations. Today, there are about 25 subgroupings within the Yoruba, but a common bond and heritage are still evident.

While the Yoruba may practice a formal religion such as Christianity or Islam, many also maintain the Yoruba ritual called Orisa. Orisa is a religion that has been practiced by the Yoruba for centuries. It has two main elements, one is play and the second is journey. "Play" is not meant in the same sense as it is in the West, as there is a seriousness tied to the idea. The elements of being spontaneous and tricking others are also tied to the Yoruba's idea of play, as there is wisdom attached to the notion. Yoruba celebrations are a wonderful place to see the Yoruba's ritual element of play. The journey refers to a person's journey through life and his or her search for personal growth and understanding of the mind and body.

Millions of Yoruba have emigrated to North America and Europe. With their migration, they have diffused or carried elements of their culture thereby enriching their new communities. Some Yoruba were forced as slaves to British, French, Portuguese, and Spanish colonies in the New World. Crowded into European slave ships, many died en route as a result of horrible conditions that prevailed in the slave trade.

Clothing in Nigeria is extremely regional, with distinctive dress often being associated with particular ethnic groups. For example, the colorful headpiece for women is called a *gela* in the Yoruba language. A variety of headpieces can be created by women from a colorful rectangular piece of cloth. Both men and women may wear a *buba*, which is a long loose-fitting shirt or blouse. For men the headpiece, a *fila*, is a small cap that fits on the head. On special occasions, men may also wear a traditional loose-fitting floor-length Yoruba article of clothing called an *agbada*. Both the traditional clothing of men and women are very bright, colorful, and elegant.

IBO

Imagine entering a school or business for a social or business meeting, or having been invited as a guest into a home in southeastern Nigeria. At the beginning of the gathering you are offered a kola nut. What do you do next? Or imagine that a collection of money has been gathered from the staff or the business people and they give you this *naira*, the Nigerian currency, during your stay. These types of ceremonies tell you that you are in Ibo country. The kola nut ceremony is a wonderful local tradition and often a humbling one for visitors (more on this later). As a visitor, perhaps you will also meet a local chief—who may be dressed in colorful local clothing, or perhaps attired in a western-style suit. Even today in many Ibo communities, a chief plays an important role in many cultural, political, and economic matters. The land of the Ibo is an exciting adventure awaiting the visitor to Nigeria.

As in many parts of Nigeria, the Ibo (also known as Igbo) have their own cultural traditions. These traditions affect song, dance, art, language, foods, clothing, and many other aspects of life. The beat of the traditional drums, with brightly dressed traditional dancers, is exciting and catches visitors in the rhythm of the music. The Ibo are also well known for the traditional masks made out of wood. These beautiful carvings reflect the strong character found in the faces of Ibo men and women who may have been the ancestors of the artist.

The Ibo reside primarily in the states of Anambra, Abia, Imo, Delta, and Cross River. Many are traders or farmers, with yams being a primary crop along with palm oil products. Historically, the Ibo split with the Yoruba a few thousand years ago, but some linguistic and other cultural patterns are similar. As with the Yoruba, there are many subculture divisions within the Ibo community.

Christianity is strong within the Ibo culture today, but traditionally they worshipped their ancestors. So that their ancestors' spirits wouldn't cause mischief, early Ibo strove to appease these spirits by observing respect at the funeral and through secret societies devoted to the departed. With this pattern of prayer for the dead, it was believed that the spirits would watch over the person and serve as an intermediate contact for God.

What about the kola nut? The kola nut ceremony, called *Oji*, is a sign that you have been welcomed into the home or business of the Ibo you have met. The Nigerians say, "He who brings kola nut brings life." Commonly used in cola drinks, the nut is offered to the oldest guest who passes the nut around to all of the others in the room. Each touches the nut as it "travels" around the group. After traveling, the nut is opened by the youngest person in the group, who also disperses the nut to everyone. Prayers for health, prosperity, safe travel, and other prayers follow the distribution of the nut. Visitors are also often given whole kola nuts to take home with them in a prayer for safe travel. The nuts are to be cracked open at home and then followed with prayer. This sign of hospitality is another example of the wonderful warmth of the Ibo people and a ceremony that has also been adopted by other cultures in Nigeria.

HAUSA

The third major cultural group in Nigeria is the Hausa who are mainly located in the north. The population resides

The traditional ruler of the Kano kingdom, the emir, participates in an annual procession called Durbar, which has been practiced since the days of an independent kingdom of Kano. On this day, the emir comes to offer prayers at the mosque and also to meet with his people. Today, the real rulers are the politicians, whether empowered by election or by a coup.

primarily in the Nigerian states of Sokoto, Kano, Bauchi, Kaduna, Zaria, and Katsina. The Hausa language and culture extends far beyond Nigeria's borders both north and westward into Niger, Benin, Ghana, and Cote D'Ivoire (formerly the Ivory Coast). Many Nigerian Fulani have also adopted the Hausa language. The vast majority of Hausa are Muslim and the culture has Arab roots that date back more than 1,000 years.

The Hausa have a long tradition of growing cotton and turning it into beautiful textiles that are traded outside of their region. Kano still serves as a city where gorgeous indigo cloth is produced. Many Hausa are subsistence farmers who depend upon the small-scale agricultural activity for survival. A variety of agricultural endeavors takes place in Hausaland, including raising livestock and growing rice, millet, corn, and a wide variety of other products. Life is tough for many Hausa as the soil is becoming less productive with the encroaching Sahara in the north and the standard of living for people in this region is lower than in the south.

By law, a Muslim man can marry up to four wives. Although Hausa men can have this many wives, economic realities frequently limit the actual number of wives a man will take. The wives are ranked in the order of their marriage to the man. Hausa society is patriarchal in nature, meaning that one's descent is traced through the man's family and name. Within the Hausa culture it is very common to talk with young people who may come from large families with 10 to 20 siblings. With up to four women in the Hausa Muslim's house, the large number of children is less surprising. Respect for one another is a high priority in the Hausa home, but the role of women tends to be more traditional and domestic and many are secluded. Even with so many traditional elements present in the Hausa home, divorce is common.

OTHER ETHNIC GROUPS

A wide variety of other ethnic groups are present in Nigeria with most existing in the central region of the country. Some may have only a few hundred people speaking the language. These cultures all contribute to the complexity of Nigeria and to the richness of diversity available for creating a greater country.

Visitors to Nigeria have many taste treats awaiting them. Local delicacies in the south include things like *jollof* rice, pepper soup, *dodo*, plantains, and a variety of yam dishes. The pounded yam is a very filling dish that will satisfy the heartiest appetite. A unique local treat is *gari*, which is made from the root of the cassava plant. It, like the pounded yam, is served along with meats, soups or other dishes, as each is very heavy. Pepper soup has a few varieties of forms as people use meat, fish, or both to add to the spicy peppery flavor of the broth. Jollof rice is also served with many different dishes and provides an important staple to the diet.

The following recipe is one that can be used for making jollof rice for six to eight people:

---

1. Cook four cups of white rice in six cups of water.

2. Do not drain the water from the rice. Add an 8-ounce can of tomato sauce and ½ can (3 ounces) of tomato paste to the cooked rice and water.

3. Add one diced onion and a diced green pepper to the mixture of rice, tomato sauce and paste.

4. Cook mixture for 12–15 minutes and add water as needed to allow the rice to cook fully.

5. Add salt and red pepper to taste and cook mixture until the rice is tender and ready to eat. More salt and red pepper can be added as needed.

Variations can be made to jollof rice by adding chicken or beef and using fresh tomatoes instead of the tomato sauce. Fresh red peppers create another variation in this traditional Nigerian dish.

Like pepper soup, Nigeria itself is a stew filled with many cultural ingredients. Major ingredients include the three major cultures of Ibo, Yoruba, and Hausa along with hundreds of smaller cultures. Also included are the religious ingredients of Islam, various forms of Christianity, and various animist (indigenous) beliefs. When put together, this variety can yield a tantalizing cultural mix that moves Nigeria ahead internally and within the world. When the incongruent ingredients clash, however, the stew is tainted and becomes unpalatable. Thus, these clashes impact not only the present, but also the near future as time is then required to heal the wounds of these divisions.

Olusegun Obasanjo has served Nigeria twice as president. He was first put in place by a military coup and second, almost 20 years later, by election.

7

Nigerian Government and Politics

"If men were angels, there would be no need for government." This quote from American President James Madison rings perhaps more true for Nigeria than for most other countries. Torn apart by religious and ethnic divisions, government has served as both a bond and as a system of justice for a society that is often fragmented and unjust. At other times, under some military leaders, it has been an abusive system where people suffered under the rule of men, rather than the rule of law, and corruption served as a cancer gnawing away at the very body of Nigerian society.

Controlled by the British until gaining independence on October 1, 1960, Nigeria had to wait a long time for self-rule. When self-rule came, it was a very bumpy trip with the military frequently interrupting short periods of civilian rule. The struggle between military and civilian rule has become legendary and has brought with it both cruel dictators and enlightened democratic rulers.

The following chart demonstrates the common and frequently violent transitions of government. It identifies each leader since independence was gained, his time in office, the way he left office, and whether he was a military or civilian leader.

NIGERIAN GOVERNMENT LEADERS

Name	Military or Civilian	Time in Office	How Left Office
Tafawa Balewa	Civilian	6 years	Killed in coup
Johnson Aguiyi-Ironsi	Military	6 months	Killed in coup
Yakubu Gowan	Military	9 years	Left in coup
Murtala Muhammed	Military	7 months	Killed in failed coup
Olusegun Obasanjo	Military	3½ years	Left voluntarily
Shehu Shagari	Civilian	4 years	Military coup
Mohammed Bahari	Military	1⅔ years	Military coup
Ibrihim Babangida	Military	8 years	Resigned from office
Ernest Shonekan	Civilian	3 months	Military coup
Sani Abacha	Military	4½ years	Died of heart attack
Abdulsalan Abubakar	Military	1 year	Left voluntarily
Olusegun Obasanjo	Civilian	1999–?	

Olusegun Obasanjo, who led Nigeria in the late 1970s, is the same person serving as the elected president at the beginning of the twenty-first century. He gained great popularity by handing the government back to civilian rule with a new constitution in 1979 after 12 years of military rule. Thus, when the country returned to civilian-led government under the present constitution of 1999 and Nigeria again looked for a democratic leader, voters turned to Obasanjo. In March 2003, in a hotly contested and violence-marred election, Obasanjo was reelected with 62 percent of the vote. Election monitors reported many cases of stolen ballot boxes, fraudulent vote counts, polling-booth intimidation, buying of votes, and many other problems. Throughout the country, more than 35 people died as a result of election-related violence. Whereas the Muslim-dominated northern opposition called the voting a "huge joke," others saw the election as an important test of stability and democracy.

THE GOVERNMENT OF NIGERIA

Nigeria's current constitution and government are relatively new, as the new constitution was implemented in 1999. The constitution is to be supreme over all other laws in the Federal Republic of Nigeria, the official name for the country. It establishes a federal republic government with three branches. Federal means that the authority and power of government is divided between the national government and local and state governments. In a republic, power is held by the voters but exercised through their elected representatives.

The three major realms of Nigeria's government are the executive, legislative, and judicial branches. Each is created in Chapter I of the constitution, as is the designation of Abuja as the national capital. Like Washington, D.C., Abuja is not contained within a state. Rather, it holds a separate political status as the Federal Capital Territory. Abuja is a recent

Today's federal government is centered in the capital of Abuja. One legacy of British colonial rule is a huge government bureaucracy. One African way of circumventing the bureaucracy has been the practice of bribery. The government is working hard to eliminate this corrupt tradition.

capital. Historically, Lagos held this function, until it was moved to the new city in December 1991.

THREE BRANCHES OF GOVERNMENT

Nigeria's executive branch is headed by an elected president and vice president who becomes president if the individual elected to that office can no longer function in that capacity. The legislative branch is called the National Assembly. It is composed of two houses called the Senate and House of Representatives, as in the United States. The judicial branch is the third branch and serves as the Nigerian federal court system.

Powers of the president and the executive branch are strong in Nigeria. This is not surprising when one considers the strong military and civilian executives who have influenced the country's history. The executive branch also has a cabinet of advisors who are appointed by the president to administer various federal government departments. The head of each cabinet department is called a minister and the agency they head is called a ministry. There are over 25 ministries in Nigeria and they include departments for education, commerce, defense, justice, finance, petroleum resources, health, and the environment. There is even a Ministry of Women Affairs and Youth Development.

Chapter VI of Nigeria's constitution outlines the requirements, responsibilities, and limitations of the presidency and executive branch. The president is the chief executive officer of the country and the commander-in-chief of the military. Under this constitution, as is true in most democracies, a civilian heads the military. There are four requirements for being elected president. The person must be at least 40 years old, a member of a political party, a citizen of Nigeria by birth, and educated up to the school certificate level (comparable to high-school graduate in the United States). Surprisingly, the constitution lists all of the presidential requirements with the male reference "he," such as "he is a citizen of Nigeria by birth." This reference is particularly strange inasmuch as the constitution clearly states that there is gender equality, which means that a woman can be elected to the presidency. Another rather unique requirement is the attainment of an educational certificate. This provision appears to discriminate against the poor and also women, many of whom receive less education.

The president is elected to a four-year term of office and the vice president succeeds the president if the individual dies, is impeached, or is not able to conduct the responsibilities of the office. He has many powers including making numerous important appointments and agreeing or not agreeing with pieces of legislation that are brought forward from the National Assembly. He is also head of the military and may pardon criminals who are serving time in prison. The president serves as the national spokesperson for Nigeria and this role is very important given the importance of Nigeria in Africa and increasingly as an important modern world nation.

Members of the National Assembly are elected by the citizens of their district or state, with all registered persons 18 and older eligible to vote. Each state elects three senators and one senator is elected from the Federal Capital Territory of Abuja. Members of the House of Representatives are elected from districts based on population, much like the U.S. House of Representatives. There are 360 members of the House of Representatives. The speaker of the House presides over the House of Representatives and the president of the Senate presides over the Senate.

Members of the Senate must be at least 35 years of age, while members of the House must be at least 30. All members of the National Assembly must be a member of a political party and possess a school graduation certificate or its equivalent. A person may not be a member if he or she fails to meet certain qualifications. Disqualifications include being a citizen of another nation; being judged a lunatic (the word lunatic is actually used in the constitution); holding membership in a secret society; being bankrupt; or awaiting a court-imposed death sentence. Members of the National Assembly are elected for four-year terms.

The National Assembly meets for at least 181 days each year in Abuja and is responsible for making laws. Bills can be introduced in either the House or the Senate and, when agreed to by the president, become laws. The president has 30 days to act on bills that arrive for his assent. If the president fails to act, or disagrees with the bill, a two-thirds majority of both houses can still pass the bill into law without his agreement. If the Senate and House disagree on a bill, they can create a conference committee to work out a compromise on the proposed legislation.

Chapter VII of Nigeria's constitution establishes the Supreme Court of Nigeria, as well as other lower courts. The Supreme Court has a chief justice and may have as many as 21 justices, although as few as 5 can actually make a decision. The National Assembly sets the actual number of justices. Justices are appointed by the president, but must also be approved by a majority of the Senate.

The Supreme Court has original jurisdiction in two types of cases. Original jurisdiction means that the case under consideration is being heard for the first time. It can only take first-time cases in disagreements between states or in cases between the national government and states. However, the National Assembly has the power to increase the type of original cases heard by the Supreme Court. Other cases come to the Supreme Court from the Court of Appeals, or other lower courts.

Lower courts are established at the national and state levels with Sharia law courts even existing in many northern states. Cases from these Sharia courts may also be reviewed by the Court of Appeals and possibly even the Supreme Court if needed. However, the Supreme Court is the highest court in the land and its decisions are final unless the constitution is changed. This means that the Supreme Court can reverse decisions of Sharia courts—a factor that occasionally causes conflict in Nigeria.

A hotly contested political point between the Muslim north and the Christian south is the introduction of Sharia Islamic law in the late 1990s. The courts mete out comparatively strict justice based on the Koran, which many believe is unfair to non-Muslims.

RIGHTS AND RESPONSIBILITIES OF CITIZENS

Democratic governments are built on the involvement of citizens. Nigeria's citizens are new to democracy, but have a large role to play in the success of the new constitution and government. Passive citizen engagement opens the door for a military coup, or other authoritarian rulers to step in and return the country to a dictatorship.

What are the rights guaranteed to the citizens of Nigeria in their constitution? First, the constitution grants the right to life. This means that all citizens are entitled to live unless sentenced to death by a court. In many societies this right gets lost and seems unimportant. In Nigeria, however, life under previous governments has often been precarious and this constitutional guarantee keeps this right sacred. Other major rights of citizens protected by Nigeria's constitution include:

- The right to privacy in communications and in their home.

- Freedom of thought, conscience, and religion.

- Freedom of expression. This includes the right to speak freely without harming others and implies a freedom of the press and media.

- Freedom of assembly and association meaning the right to form groups whether they are political or nonpolitical.

- Freedom of movement within Nigeria. This means that people can freely move and live where they want.

- The right to own property.

- The right to a fair trial. This includes such things as the right to have legal representation and the assumption that a person is innocent until proven guilty.

Citizens are also protected in the constitution from torture, slavery, and inhumane treatment. Equality is promoted for all citizens regardless of ethnic group, gender, religion, disability, or any other status. With all of the religious and ethnic tensions existing in the country the enforcement of these rights is a very important—and often difficult—function of the national government.

Citizens also have responsibilities. In many nations these duties are assumed, but in Nigeria they are specifically spelled out in the constitution in Chapter II, Section 24 which states:

"It shall be the duty of every citizen to—

(a) abide by this Constitution, respect its ideals and its institutions, the National Flag, the National Anthem, the National Pledge, and legitimate authorities;

(b) help to enhance the power, prestige and good name of Nigeria, defend Nigeria and render such national service as may be required;

(c) respect the dignity of other citizens and the rights and legitimate interests of others and live in unity and harmony and in the spirit of common brotherhood;

(d) make positive and useful contributions to the advancement, progress and well-being of the community where he resides;

(e) render assistance to appropriate and lawful agencies in the maintenance of law and order; and

(f) declare his income honestly to appropriate and lawful agencies and pay his tax promptly.

Nigeria requires a strong national government to effectively govern this diverse and conflicted society. With the strong religious divisions between the north and south, the potential for governmental conflict with Sharia law and courts has provided many dramatic cases already. Each of these cases has reinforced the supremacy of the 1999 constitution and the authority of the president, National Assembly, and the Supreme Court. That more cases will arise is a certainty as some individuals and groups hope to erode the democratic government that presently exists.

Like the Pledge of Allegiance in the United States, Nigeria also has a National Pledge for citizens. Notice how unity is prominently stated in the effort to remind citizens of the vital need for a national identity.

"I pledge to Nigeria my country

To be faithful, loyal, and honest

To serve Nigeria with all my strength

To defend her unity and uphold her honor and glory

So help me God."

Once a food exporter, Nigeria must now import tons of food daily to feed its people. The huge resulting debt focuses the country's economy on its cash exports of petroleum and gas. This leaves few jobs for ordinary people who turn to selling items on the streets.

8

Nigeria's Economy

I t is a hot, sticky afternoon in Lagos. The time is about 4:30 P.M.
and vehicles are crawling along in a traffic jam that Nigerians
call a "slow go." A major cause of the slow go is the hundreds
of children and adults floating from car to car to sell the products
they are lugging with them in traffic. Darting in and out between
vehicles, the sellers hawk a virtual superstore array of food, clothing,
compact discs, water, magazines, cooking utensils, and hundreds
of other household goods. Children as young as five also danger-
ously drift from one driver to the next to make a sale. This traffic
situation provides visitors with an early introduction to the day-
to-day economy of Nigeria, where thousands of people work on
the streets, or in small roadside stands, to sell all of the necessities
of life to other Nigerians.

Nigeria's economy is moving forward very slowly. Most of the economy is driven by simple daily transactions between buyers and sellers such as those described above. In contrast, Nigeria is also a great oil-producing country. Although rich in "black gold," Nigeria frequently suffers from severe gasoline shortages. Why? Corruption is the main reason, as this seamy side of Nigerian society robs the nation of its true economic potential in oil and in many other areas of the economy.

Unemployment runs high, with nearly 30 percent of the population falling into this category. Many more are under-employed, that is, they hold jobs that offer very low wages or are only part-time. Only about a third of the land is arable, or suitable for farming. With a rapidly expanding population, Nigeria finds that it cannot now feed itself and must import food. Food imports drain much-needed hard currencies, such as the U.S. dollar or the European Euro, from the country.

Other problems facing Nigeria's economy are rising inflation and a very large foreign debt owed to other nations. These elements add weight to the other challenges facing the economy.

ECONOMIC ACTIVITY IN NIGERIA

Agriculture had been the mainstay of Nigeria for decades until the 1960s when petroleum became the country's chief economic contributor. This newfound wealth allowed Nigeria to import products and raw materials from other countries, as oil prices rose in the early 1970s because of the oil embargo imposed by the Organization of the Petroleum Exporting Nations (OPEC). Nigeria joined OPEC in 1971. At the same, the oil boom led to increased government spending and inflation that ultimately led to increased unemployment.

A severe drought plagued Nigeria in 1972 and 1974 and the resulting food shortages caused starvation in Nigeria and other African nations. Immigration because of the famine caused more Africans to move into Nigeria, making the problem even larger.

In the mid-1970s, the naira, Nigeria's currency, experienced a big decline in value. This meant that inflation was eating away at the buying power of citizens. Because of the high inflation rate, the cost to borrow money also rose as banks charged high interest rates. These events discouraged people from starting businesses. At the same time, Nigeria had been limiting the amount of foreign investment in local businesses. Sharp economic decline created an economic nightmare at a time when the country's population was undergoing a rapid increase.

Having an oil industry usually means that environmentally conscious citizens watch over the industry to protect the environment. By the late 1990s, oil production remained high, but protesting environmentalists were persecuted harshly by Sani Abacha, Nigeria's leader at the time. Many of these protesters were even killed by the leader's henchmen. After Abacha's death in 1998, protesters conducted activities that resulted in large decreases in oil production. In 2002, women in the Niger Delta took political action, protesting the fact that few Nigerians were hired by the oil companies to work in the industry. This resulted in the companies promising to hire more local people.

Agriculture

Over half of Nigeria's population is engaged in agriculture. A wide variety of items are produced, including such things as cocoa, peanuts, yams, corn, palm oil, rice, sorghum, millet, and rubber. Animals raised for agricultural purposes include cattle sheep, pigs, and goats. Fishing is another key industry and cities like Lagos and Port Harcourt have extensive fishing industries.

In the 1960s, before the discovery of oil, Nigeria was an exporter of food which accounted for over two-thirds of the country's exports at that time. Sadly, today Nigeria is an importer of food products, a factor that costs the nation millions of dollars in hard currency that the nation finds in short supply. Importing food has also added to the substantial debts that Nigeria owes to other nations.

Manufacturing

Most manufacturing in Nigeria takes place in small factories, or even in homes where people produce various products. Nigeria has been named one of the world's most corrupt countries. It also has a history of political instability and today carries a huge foreign debt. For these and perhaps other reasons, few international companies choose to invest in Nigeria, where investment carries extra risk. Despite the lack of foreign investment, some of the major items produced include textiles, cement and other construction materials, steel, printing, and various food products.

Natural Resources

Oil is king in Nigeria. This resource represents over 90 percent of the country's exports and is a key source for obtaining foreign hard currency (the Nigerian currency, the naira, is not used internationally). Over 2,100,000 barrels of oil are produced each day from some 250 small fields in the Niger Delta. Nigeria's oil production amounts to only 3 to 4 percent of the world total. Even this relatively small amount, though, is of great importance in a country otherwise lacking any major source of revenue. Unfortunately, however, the oil production is closely tied to rampant corruption. Much of the country's production is spirited away in black-market operations that smuggle millions of dollars of revenue from the country. Fraud and kickbacks still plague the industry even though recent efforts have been made to stop corruption. Government officials have often been the ones most deeply involved in oil smuggling, thereby depriving their fellow citizens of money that would help alleviate Nigeria's widespread poverty and the large debts owed to other nations.

The center of Nigeria's oil region is in the south in the Niger River delta region. Port Harcourt, located on the Gulf of Guinea, is the city that serves as the hub of the oil region. Two

Workers on an oil rig off the shore of Nigeria help produce the "black gold" that has become the salvation of the impoverished nation.

of the four oil refineries in Nigeria, Port Harcourt I and II, are located in Port Harcourt. Because of the oil wealth, living in the city is more expensive than most other places in Nigeria.

Tourism

Although Nigeria has a number of places that should be attractive to tourists, few people are drawn to the country in that role. Even though law enforcement agencies are making progress in addressing these problems, corruption and violence discourage most potential visitors. Thus, the economic impact of tourism to Nigeria is minimal.

Only limited accommodations are suitable for visitors. Abuja has a "world-class" hotel, but few clean, comfortable, and safe lodging facilities can be found outside of the major cities. Tour companies and other agencies or facilities designed to assist the visitor are also very limited.

ENERGY

Nigeria's location provides it with a climate that rarely requires heating. This is fortunate, because most Nigerians live in very austere homes that require little electricity. Cooking is often done over an open flame. Many homes and schools still do not even have electricity. All nations need energy and in Nigeria oil is the primary source.

Even when electricity is present in Nigeria, there are frequent power outages. Most large businesses have their own generators to provide electricity when the power goes out. Nigeria has three hydroelectric power stations and five thermal (oil-powered) power stations. Yet despite these facilities, the actual production of electricity has declined during recent years. Today, most Nigerians do not have access to electricity. In fact, only 40 percent of the country's people have access to power and in rural areas the figure drops to only 10 percent.

To address the shortage of electricity, Nigeria is planning to have small, independent, privately owned power producers play a larger role in the marketplace. This will end the practice of electrical production as a government monopoly and will promote some competition. Nigeria's national electrical power agency has set a goal of having 85 percent of the people supplied with electricity in 2010.

TRANSPORTATION

Traveling to and from Nigeria is not always an easy task. Because most Nigerians lack the financial means to travel abroad, there are few international flights. Lagos, Port Harcourt, and the capital city of Abuja contain the primary international airports with Lagos being the most important. From Nigeria, there are airline connections to Paris, London, Amsterdam, Geneva, Frankfort, and several other major cities in Europe. No flights connect Nigeria directly with cities in North America and a traveler must connect through Europe, or other places in Africa. Nigeria is also connected by air to a few African countries, including Ghana, Benin, Niger, and Cameroon. However, airfare is expensive for Nigerians and air travel is a luxury few can afford.

Within the country, there are a number of local airlines that provide service. These airlines, in fact, are very competitive and provide a splendid example of the way in which a free market can bring success. Small carriers such as Belview Airlines, Nigerian Airways, Chanchangi Airlines, Kabo Airlines, Okada Air, and EAS Airlines connect Nigerian cities. Some of these airlines have only two or three planes, but competition is intense with prices sometimes even changing during the day. Lagos serves as the major hub for air traffic. Most flights go to or from Lagos, rather than connecting directly with other cities. This means that a person going from Abuja to Port Harcourt will usually travel to Lagos, switch planes, and then go to Port Harcourt on another flight.

Nigeria also has a rail system that connects some of the major cities. Unfortunately, trains tend to run sporadically and are also hampered by frequent cancellations.

Transportation on the local level varies in type and quality. It may range from motorcycles that serve as a taxicab to buses. There are the popular bush taxis, station wagons or vans that connect towns and cities across Nigeria. The local types of transportation are usually quite cheap and within the financial range of most Nigerians. The road system is good in most of the country, but can be extremely dangerous. Frequent police roadblocks slow travel in efforts to reduce crime and other

There may only be a few million private cars in Lagos, but the current infrastructure cannot handle them. New bridges and roads are badly needed in this congested city.

highway problems. Nigerian drivers contribute to an alarmingly high rate of accidents and highway fatalities.

Some more affluent Nigerians and visitors may hire cars with drivers to take them to other communities. On the highways, the drivers communicate travel information with elaborate hand signals to other drivers telling them to slow down, not to pass, or to provide other guidance.

For most Nigerians, life is lived close to home. Thus, a visitor will see thousands of people simply walking to and from shopping and other daily chores. Walking is very common and people often will go long distances by foot every day carrying water or other necessities. Distance is measured differently by most Nigerians. If you ask someone how far it is from one point to another (as from the city of Benin to Lagos) he or she is most likely to answer with travel time, rather than distance in kilometers. They will simply say "It's about three hours away," rather than "about 150 kilometers."

COMMUNICATION

Nigeria has a very poor communications infrastructure. With a rapidly increasing population, the posts, wires, and cables needed to provide telephone linkages throughout the country simply have not been able to keep pace with rising demand. The nation is too poor to create a system as in the United States. But recently Nigerians have been able to jump a generation forward in personal communication—with cell phones employing space-age technology.

TRADE

Driving by the open markets near the harbor in Port Harcourt, a visitor sees shops that offer videocassette recorders (VCRs), televisions, stereos, and many other electronic goods. All items are previously used and arrive in Port Harcourt from Europe and other locations. Since they are used, many local Nigerians can afford to purchase these electronic products for their homes. The cost of new televisions, VCRs, radios, and other products are simply too high for the average Nigerian to purchase.

As a former British colony, most Nigerian imports still come from the United Kingdom. Other countries from which Nigeria conducts extensive import trade include the United States, Japan, Brazil, and other European Union countries. Transportation equipment, petroleum products, manufactured goods, food, and machinery are leading imports.

Nigeria's economy has been transformed over the centuries from a traditional agrarian and trans-Saharan trading society to one solely based on oil production and manufacturing. The resulting 30 percent unemployment rate contributes to the widespread crime and corruption.

Nigeria's exports go primarily to the United States, European Union, Brazil, India, and Japan. Major exports include petroleum, oil products, rubber, and cocoa. Over the past four decades, leading exports have changed from agricultural commodities such as peanuts and palm oil products, to oil. Much of Nigeria's oil goes to the United States. In fact, the country is the fifth-largest supplier of this essential energy resource to the United States after Saudi Arabia, Mexico, Canada, and Venezuela.

THE ECONOMIC FUTURE

Nigeria is confronted by many economic challenges. The rapid population growth cannot be sustained by present agricultural production. Importing food and other necessities requires hard currency which, in turn, makes it more difficult for the country to pay off its huge international debts. Unpaid or late debt payments, on the other hand, keep the country from getting new loans that could be used to create jobs. Inflation decreases the value of the naira and increases the cost of goods and services. There are many challenges, but there is also cause for hope.

The greatest hope for Nigeria now appears to be the development of democratic institutions and practices. Efforts to clean up corruption have increased in recent years and have improved various aspects of the economy. Police are cracking down on violence. There is also a serious attempt to get youngsters back into school, rather than selling things on the street.

Many government-owned industries such as electricity production, hotels, telecommunications, vehicle-assembly plants, oil refineries, and paper mills are now being sold to private companies. This important step is allowing private ownership to take root in Nigeria's fragile economic soil. Many of these former government holdings are now traded as private companies on the emerging Nigerian Stock Exchange. This movement towards privatization holds promise for the future, particularly if combined successfully with a reduction in corruption.

However, much hard work is still needed to strengthen the country's economy. Today, a candle of democracy is lit in Nigeria, and many beneficial free-market advances will continue to be made if the candle continues to burn.

The flame of Nigeria, its potential, burns bright in the faces of these school-children. They are being educated and encouraged to make a difference in their homeland.

9

Nigeria's Future

Incongruent. The theme of various misfitting elements has been recurrent throughout this book about Nigeria. A variety of incongruent elements have plagued Nigeria's past and continue to do so today. As you have read, the roots of the disharmony rest deep in the country's culture and history. Some conflicts date back thousands of years, creating wounds that have not yet fully healed. Any attempt to forecast Nigeria's future must take into consideration these elements and others of more recent origin.

In March 2001, I was traveling in southern Nigeria. About 25 miles south of the city of Onitsha, a young girl perhaps 10 or 11 years old lay dead in the road. She obviously had been hit by a car and left there to die. Only a few feet away, people walked along the road and seemed not to notice the dead girl lying there. On one other occasion, I saw a man lying dead less than 50 feet from a market filled with people. In both cases the people were going along with their normal daily routine and seemed oblivious to what had happened. This is another tragic way in which Nigeria is incongruent—even in peoples' simple activities of daily life and death.

On a nationwide basis, the problems and challenges facing Nigeria today are staggering. Corruption is a major problem that has strong traditions in Nigerian political culture. This corruption not only robs the economy of badly needed money; of greater importance, perhaps, it robs the people from having a moral compass that keeps society reasonably honest and trustworthy. Widespread corruption and dishonesty robs a nation of its soul. If you cannot trust those with whom you conduct business, or even your next-door neighbor, how can a civil society be developed that will improve the common good for all people?

Another critical issue facing Nigeria is the challenge of keeping a civilian democratic government. Such a government is essential if Nigeria is to move forward and build a cohesive society with a strong national identity. The 1999 constitution seems to be a strong step in a new direction. The military has maintained a quiet role during the Obasanjo presidency. It also adopted a hands-off position during the hotly contested election of 2003. This holds promise for civilian government and rule through elected officials. The give and take of democratic governments that allow freedom of expression and other basic rights are key steps to improving Nigeria's status. The federal nature of the constitution allows local citizens to help solve public policy problems while the national government works to hold the diverse people of the country together in a fair and representative system.

Human racial, cultural, and ethnic diversity has been a source of frequent violence, including wars, in Nigeria. For the country to move forward, this challenge must be addressed and resolved. Drawing upon the resources provided by human diversity, and viewing differences as a strength rather than as a problem, can offer Nigeria resources to face the country's challenges. Intermarriage and greater mingling between individuals of differing religious and ethnic groups offer Nigeria human ties that will help to heal the scars of past wars and violence. Nigeria's human diversity can be an extremely important asset if it is developed and appropriately used as a resource of strength.

The challenge of HIV-AIDS is a growing menace in Nigeria and in all of Africa. This disease robs a nation of medical and financial resources that are already inadequate. It also takes away the human-resource potential of persons who are badly infected. AIDS education is increasing and the government has become more active in trying to slow the scourge of this disease. But it remains a huge threat to the lives and well-being of millions of Nigerians. Access to western medicines will help, but strong additional educational efforts and changes in sexual habits are needed to slow the effects of this dreaded problem.

Another critical issue facing Nigeria is the economy. Beyond addressing the problems of corruption and violence, the country must strive to diversify its economy. Oil has provided a strong economic backbone, but much more is needed. An honest, hard-working labor force could be attractive to foreign investors if they could count on political stability and honest transactions. With wages so very low, foreign investment can bring industry and jobs that will help not only the country, but also the citizens desperately in need of jobs as well.

Another issue facing Nigeria is rapid population growth. Its current population is about 130 million people, and the number grows at a current annual rate of 2.7 percent. If the current rate of growth continues, the country's population will double by 2029. It is very difficult for Nigeria's economy to keep pace with population growth. This is particularly true in regard to such essential public services as transportation, schooling, and health care. A key to holding down the rate of natural population increase is increasing the literacy rate and social status of women. This element impacts population growth in significant ways. Today, only about 47 percent of the country's women are literate. This figure must be drastically improved.

Environmental pollution and degradation also are major challenges for Nigeria. For example, in the city of Onitisha (and elsewhere), waste is scattered along roadways and throughout the city. In many places, plastic, paper, boxes, food, human waste, and other refuse is stacked three and four feet deep. Open burning of garbage leaves a horrible, hazy pall of air pollution over the city. In some cities one can actually taste the foul air. Open burning and lack of toilet facilities extend the environmental problems that cause disease and early death.

Education is an important key to a better future for Nigeria. The country needs many creative problem-solvers to address the issues mentioned in this chapter and elsewhere in this book. Today, education varies greatly. There are very adequate private schools for those students whose parents can afford them. Most Nigerian youngsters, however, attend classes in tightly cramped classrooms with 40–60 students. The poorest classrooms are open to the elements, have no maps or other instructional information on the bare walls, and no books or writing materials for children. Teachers do the best that they can, but are paid very little for their work. One of the primary potential contributors to a better Nigeria, education, also faces many challenges. These students, after all, represent the best hope for the country's future.

The importance of Nigeria in Africa, and especially West Africa, is very great. As Africa's most populated nation, the country can provide much-needed regional leadership. Among Nigeria's people, there are emerging new leaders who view the country in a much different way than people have in the past. Formerly seen as two or more regions, new leaders are taking a more holistic approach. Civic education is beginning to take root, working to help citizens and students understand how they are important in a democracy. Special courses are providing them with the background and experiences necessary to become active and contributing citizens.

Remember the little girl who died in the road? Only the day before in Onitisha, the violent polluted city of over a million people, students were working to develop a new public policy. High-school students at Creative Minds Foundation School developed a public policy recommendation that would make street and road crossings safer. The work of these students was put into law in late May 2001. The result was "zebra" markings being painted at appropriate locations on all of the roads in the state in order that pedestrians could safely cross. This was the first time that students in Nigeria were responsible for developing and lobbying for a new law that was implemented by their government. They had benefited from civic education received from a program called "Project Citizen," developed by the Center for Civic Education in the United States.

There is hope. When you look into the eyes of young Nigerians and emerging political leaders, you see hope. I heard students in Bishop Lasbury School in the south sing "We are the chosen generation." With the belief in this phrase and the energy and intelligence behind it, Nigeria can have a bright and shining future. But it will take the hard work and the cooperation of all Nigerians.

Nigeria's national motto sums up the country's hope for the future: "Peace and Unity, Strength and Progress."

Facts at a Glance

Country Name	Federal Republic of Nigeria
Location	West Africa, bordering the Gulf of Guinea, between Benin and Cameroon, southwest of Chad, and south of Niger
Capital	Abuja
Area	356,700 square miles (923,770 square kilometers)
Land Features	Southern lowlands; hills and plateaus in central region; mountains in southeast; plains in the north
Climate	Equatorial in south, tropical in the central region, arid in the north
Major Water Features	Gulf of Guinea coastline, Niger River, Benue River, Lake Chad in northeast
Natural Hazards	Floods, droughts
Land Use	Arable land: 33%
	Permanent crops: 3%
	Other: 64%
Environmental Issues	Degraded soil, deforestation, air and water pollution, desertification, rapid urbanization
Population	129,934,911 (July 2002 estimate)
Population Growth Rate	2.54% per year
Total Fertility Rate	5.49 (average number of children born to each woman during childbearing years)
Life Expectancy at Birth	50 ½ years (same for males and females)
HIV-AIDS Prevalence Rate	5.06%
Ethnic Groups	Hausa-Fulani, 29%, Yoruba, 21%; Ibo, 18%; Ijaw, 10%, other, 22%
Religion	Muslim, 50%; Christian, 40%; indigenous religions, 10%
Languages	English is the official language, Hausa, Yoruba, Ibo, Fulani, Ijaw, Tiv, and over 200 other languages
Literacy	Total population, 57.1%; male, 67.3%; female, 47.3%
Type of Government	Federal republic
Executive Branch	Chief of State (elected by citizens)

Legislative Branch	National Assembly (two houses, Senate and House of Representatives)
Independence	October 1, 1960
Administrative Divisions	36 states, Federal Territory of Abuja
Currency	Naira
Labor Force by Occupation	Agriculture, 70%; industry, 10%; services, 20%
Industries	Crude oil, coal, palm oil, peanuts, cotton, rubber, wood, leathergoods, textiles, cement, food products, footwear, chemicals, fertilizer, tin, steel
Primary Exports	Petroleum and petroleum products, cocoa, rubber
Export Partners	United States, Spain, India, France, Brazil
Imports	Machinery, chemicals, manufactured goods, transportation equipment, food, and animals.
Import Partners	United Kingdom, United States, France, Germany, China

History at a Glance

8000 B.C.	First human remains date back to this time
3000	Agriculture emerges in the south of Nigeria
400	Nok culture begins
200 A.D.	Demise of the Nok culture
998	Kingdom of Kano created
1000	Kanem and Borno kingdoms develop in northeast Nigeria
1000	Trade routes across Sahara Desert begin developing from northern Nigeria
1471	Portuguese explore the Niger River delta
1480s	Portuguese begin trading with the kingdom of Benin
1807	British Parliament bans British citizens from slave trade
1820s	Oyo kingdom falls leaving Aro as the leading African slave trading state
1861	British annex Lagos
1870	Slavery is abolished
1902	British seize Kano
1914	Nigeria made a British colony
1939–1945	Nigeria fights for Allies in World War II
1960	Nigeria gains independence from the United Kingdom; First Republic is created; Nigeria joins the United Nations
1963	Nigeria becomes a member of the British Commonwealth
1966	Nigerian military stages its first coup under General Ironsi; the civilian government is removed
1967	Eastern Nigeria secedes from Nigeria under Lieutenant Colonel Ojukwu and forms Biafra; civil war follows
1970	Biafra War ends with the defeat of Biafra's forces; starvation follows in that region
1979	Civilian rule and the start of the Second Republic; Shehu Shagari assumes presidency
1983	End of the Second Republic; military coup installs General Mohammed Bahari as leader
1985	General Bahari overthrown in a military coup, General Ibrahim Babangida becomes leader

1986 Wole Soyinka, a Nigerian writer, becomes the first African to win the Nobel Prize

1999 Nigeria adopts present constitution establishing the Third Republic; Olusegun Obasanjo is elected president

2001 Hundreds die in religious violence and fighting in the north related to September 11, 2001, attack on the World Trade Centers in United States

2002 Hundreds die in violence in the north and Abuja related to the Miss World Pageant

2003 Olusengun Obasanjo reelected to presidency in hotly contested election

Further Reading

Achebe, Chinua. *Home and Exile.* New York, NY: Oxford University Press, 2000.

Achebe, Chinua. *Things Fall Apart.* Anchor Books, October, 1994.

Achebe, Chinua. *Trouble with Nigeria.* Heinemann, 1984.

Aguwa, Jude C. *Agriculture and Modernity in Nigeria: A Historical and Contemporary Survey of the Igbo Experience.* Triatlantic Books Ltd., 1998.

Badru, Pade. *Imperialism and Ethnic Politics in Nigeria, 1960-96.* Africa World Press, 1998.

Davidson, Basil. *Let Freedom Come: Africa in Modern History.* Boston, MA: Little, Brown and Company, 1978.

Fage, J.D. *A History of West Africa.* New York, NY: Cambridge University Press, 1972.

Falola, Toyin. *Culture and Customs of Nigeria (Culture and Customs of Africa).* Greenwood Publishing Group, 2000.

Falola, Toyin. *The History of Nigeria (Greenwood Histories of the Modern Nations).* Greenwood Publishing Group, 1999.

Falola, Toyin. *Violence in Nigeria: The Crisis of Religious Politics and Secular Ideologies.* University of Rochester Press, 2001.

Hamilton, Janice. *Nigeria in Pictures (Visual Geography Series).* Lerner Publications Company, 2003.

Iioeje, Nwadilibe P. *New Geography of Nigeria.* Longman, 1976.

Isichei, Elizabeth. *Studies in the History of Plateau State, Nigeria.* MacMillan Pub. Ltd. 1982.

Jones, G.I. *The Trading States of the Oil Rivers: A Study of Political Development in Eastern Nigeria.* Lit Verlag, 2001.

Koslow, Philip. *Hausaland: The Fortress Kingdoms.* Bt Bound, October, 1999.

Koslow, Philip. *Yorubaland: The Flowering of Genius (Kingdoms of Africa).* Chelsea House Pub., 1996.

Lamb, David. *The Africans.* New York, NY: Random House, 1982.

Maier, Karl. *This House Has Fallen: Midnight in Nigeria.* New York, NY: Public Affairs, 2000.

Mbeke-Ekanem, Tom and Nyong, Frances E. *Beyond the Execution: Understanding The Ethnic and Military Politics in Nigeria.* Writer's Showcase Press, 2000.

Murray, Jocelyn (Editor). *Cultural Atlas of Africa.* New York, NY: Checkmark Books, 1998.

Nnoromele, Salome and Goodwin, William. *Nigeria (Modern Nations of the World).* Lucent Books, 2001.

Okome, Mojubaolu Olufunke. *A Sapped Democracy.* University Press of America, 1998.

Olanijan, Richard (Editor). *Nigerian History and Culture.* Longman Group United Kingdom, 1985.

Osaghae, Eghosa E. *Crippled Giant: Nigeria Since Independence.* Bloomington, Indiana: Indiana University Press, 1998.

Oyewole, Anthony and Lucas, John. *Historical Dictionary of Nigeria.* Scarecrow Press, 2000.

Schraeder, Peter J. *African Politics and Society: A Mosaic in Transformation.* Boston, MA: Bedford/St. Martin's, 2000.

Schultz, John Frederick (Editor). *Nigeria in Pictures (Visual Geography Series).* Lerner Publications Company, 1995.

Soyinka, Wole. *The Open Sore of a Continent: A Personal Narrative of the Nigerian Crisis (The W.E.B. Dubois Institute Series).* New York, NY: Oxford University Press, 1997.

Suberu, Rotimi T. *Federalism and Ethnic Conflict in Nigeria.* United States Institute of Peace, 2001.

Uchendu, Victor Chikezie. *The Igbo of Southeast Nigeria.* International Thomson Publishing, 1965.

Index

Index

Index

Index

page:

8:	New Millennium Images	55:	AFP/NMI
11:	© 2003 maps.com	58:	AFP/NMI
13:	KRT/NMI	62:	Saurabh Das/AP/Wide World Photos
16:	New Millennium Images	64:	AFP/NMI
19:	© 2003 maps.com	70:	Saurabh Das/AP/Wide World Photos
23:	KRT/NMI	74:	AFP/NMI
25:	KRT/NMI	78:	KRT/NMI
28:	AFP/NMI	82:	AFP/NMI
31:	© Daniel Laine/CORBIS	86:	KRT/NMI
35:	© Bettmann/CORBIS	91:	AFP/NMI
38:	New Millennium Images	94:	AFP/NMI
40:	© Hulton-Deutsch Collection/CORBIS	96:	AFP/NMI
47:	© Hulton-Deutsch Collection/CORBIS	98:	KRT/NMI
50:	AFP/NMI		

Cover: © Paul Almasy/CORBIS

About the Author

DOUGLAS A. PHILLIPS is a lifetime educator and writer who has traveled to over 75 countries. During his career he has worked as a middle school teacher, and as a curriculum developer, writer, and trainer of educators around the world. He has served as the President of the National Council for Geographic Education and has received the Outstanding Service Award from the National Council for the Social Studies along with numerous other awards. He, his wife Marlene, and their three children, Chris, Angela, and Daniel have lived in South Dakota and Alaska but now he and his family reside in Arizona where he writes and serves as an educational consultant for the Center for Civic Education and other educational entities. He has worked and traveled extensively in Nigeria and has met with political and educational leaders, teachers, and students in efforts designed to promote civic education in the country. He dedicates this book to the Nigerian educators and youth who are working to develop new democratic values and traditions in Africa's most populated nation.

CHARLES F. ("FRITZ") GRITZNER is Distinguished Professor of Geography at South Dakota University in Brookings. He is now in his fifth decade of college teaching and research. During his career, he has taught more than 60 different courses, spanning the fields of physical, cultural, and regional geography. In addition to his teaching, he enjoys writing, working with teachers, and sharing his love for geography with students. As consulting editor for the MODERN WORLD NATIONS series, he has a wonderful opportunity to combine each of these "hobbies." Fritz has served as both president and executive director of the National Council for Geographic Education and has received the Council's highest honor, the George J. Miller Award for Distinguished Service.